THE
ELEGANT
PEASANT

THE
ELEGANT PEASANT

MARGUERITE THOMAS

happy eating —
love, Marguerite
Oct. 1984

JEREMY P. TARCHER, INC.
Los Angeles

Distributed by St. Martin's Press
New York

To Frank S. Jewett

Library of Congress Cataloging in Publication Data

Thomas, Marguerite
   The elegant peasant.

   Includes index.
     1. Cookery, International.   2. Peasantry.
I. Title.
TX725.A1T49 1987   641.59   86-22998
ISBN 0-87477-417-9

Jeremy P. Tarcher, Inc.
9110 Sunset Blvd.
Los Angeles, CA 90069

Design by Thom Dower
Illustration by Rosanne Litzinger

Manufactured in the United States of America
10 9 8 7 6 5 4 3 2 1

First Edition

CONTENTS

CONTENTS

ACKNOWLEDGMENTS

With special thanks to my agent, Charlotte Sheedy, for her belief in the idea and her help in making it a reality, and to my editor, Janice Gallagher, for her ideas, skills, enthusiasm, and critical suggestions. I would also like to express my thanks to the Warner Library in Tarrytown, New York, for providing a handsome, helpful, and peaceful place to write.

INTRODUCTION: THE PEASANT "UPRISING"

Until the Industrial Revolution, the world was made up mostly of peasants. There were starving peasants and sleek, well-fed peasants, Japanese peasants and Spanish peasants, grim-faced peasants and peasants who enjoyed a rollicking good time like the ones in Bruegel's paintings. Some peasants were free small landowners, some were hired laborers. What they all had in common—as the root *pais,* the old French word for country, indicates—was a connection to the land. Ninety percent of the pre-Industrial population lived in a rural society and had a stake in an agrarian economy. Most people's work was related to agriculture. And almost everyone subsisted on a peasant diet.

Of course, there are great differences between one culture's peasant cuisine and the next. Some people eat rice while in another country corn is the staple. One man's meat may be another nation's taboo. In certain communities food is grilled over fire whereas others boil it in a kettle, depending on available sources of fuel. There are, however, many common denominators. Peasants have not generally been able to afford as much meat as their more affluent brethren in the nobility and bourgeoisie; their meals are based on a grain or legume, such as rice, beans, wheat, or corn, augmented by small amounts of animal protein (meat, fish, eggs, or dairy products) rather than the other way around. The traditional peasant diet is relatively low in fats: although vegetable oils are used extensively in many peasant cultures, cream and butter seldom predominate. Simple fruit-based desserts are more common in peasant homes than are highly sweetened and elaborate baked goods.

Peasant cooking, like any other cooking, is based on tradition. But the peasant world was a world in flux: throughout history waves of armies rolled regularly over the countryside, trade routes crisscrossed land and sea, pilgrims and crusaders pursued their sometimes elusive goals to the corners of the world. Through means such as these, ideas and goods were transported around the world, bringing change to even the most entrenched traditions.

Food began moving between cultures very early on. In the eighteenth century B.C. nomadic Asians brought the first olives to Egypt. Egypt supplied ancient Rome with grain for its bread. Roman soldiers took leeks to the British Isles, and British Pilgrims introduced apples to the New World. The New World provided tomatoes and potatoes to be taken back to Europe by Spanish conquistadors; on a return trip the Spaniards brought the first sugarcane, which they got from the Arabs, to the West Indies. The Arabs went to China and discovered cinnamon, while the Chinese brought oranges to India. And so it went, round and round the globe, with new ingredients making their way sooner or later into traditional peasant cooking pots.

With the Industrial Revolution came the gradual erosion of peasant culture. As masses of people shifted from fields to factories, abandoning tradition-bound village communities for the relatively formless structure of urban life, most of the habits, beliefs, customs, and conventions that had evolved over hundreds of generations disappeared. Certainly eating habits changed radically. In the move from farm to city and suburb, regional recipes and native products vanished along with the emphasis on fresh fruits and vegetables, grains, legumes, and cheeses that had characterized the peasant diet. Which is not to say that many of the changes weren't for the better: the past two hundred years have brought a certain amount of relief, at least in the Western world, to the devastating episodes of famine and drought that swept periodically over the peasantry. The limited and bland diet that most of the world's peasants subsisted on has improved in many ways. But along with the improvements much was lost, for in spite of severe flaws, peasant cooking had delicious virtues. It was distinctive. It had character. It reflected regional and individual personality. At its best, peasant food was fresh and nutritious.

Today, by a curious quirk of twentieth-century circumstances, our own eating habits mirror some of the finer qualities of peasant cooking. We've rediscovered a passion for very fresh foods directly from the land or sea rather than packaged, canned, or frozen. We've developed a genuine interest in foods from other nations. And we're even acquiring a taste for American regional foods—Cajun cooking, Southwestern ingredients, Southern and soul foods.

Writers such as James Beard and M.F.K. Fisher began the sharpening of America's native gastronomic intellect, and Julia Child made *cuisine* a household word. Michel Guerard taught us that fine cooking didn't have to make us fat. Our outlook became more international as more and more Americans traveled for business and pleasure. Mass-media communication has fanned an international passion for foods from other cultures, and technological improvements in refrigeration and transportation allow us to enjoy fresh foods that have been whisked to us across the globe. The top chefs in America today—people such as Alice Waters, Wolfgang Puck, Jonathan Waxman—are, by and large, well educated in the arts and humanities, which may be part of the reasons why their attitude toward food and cooking is characterized by imagination and daring as well as a high level of expertise. They have undergone apprenticeship in international settings where they developed a reverence for traditional fare as well as enthusiasm for contemporary techniques.

My own background, I think, is representative of today's attitude toward food. Raised and educated in both France and California, my heart, head, and taste buds are equally addicted to both places; overlapping cultures seem the normal state of affairs to me. I've interpreted classes for American students at the Cordon Bleu in Paris and taught French literature in California universities. For years I conducted classes, alternate semesters, in French cooking and California food and wines. Living and eating in Manhattan for the past few years, and traveling to Europe occasionally, have given me the opportunity to taste what contemporary chefs are excited about, and to have my own notions reconfirmed that good food and good eating overlap national boundaries more than ever before.

During recent visits to the west coast of Ireland and to rural Belgium, for example, I found the same spirit of freshness, lightness, and innovation as in Paris and London, although the interpretation was different in each country. Regional and national traditions are valued but not treated with undue reverence. Why shouldn't homey lasagne noodles be partnered with a delicate Marsala-flavored chicken for a

3

change, or stewy beef shanks be perked up with fresh ginger, borrowed from Oriental cuisine? I don't see why carbonnade, that wonderful beer and onion–based Belgian stew, always has to have the beef simmered in it for hours; quickly cooked slices of tenderloin profit from the sturdy flavors, too, especially with brioches to help soak up the sauce.

This is where the "elegant" part of this book comes in, to describe the juxtaposition of twentieth-century standards with traditional fare. It is an attitude about cooking and eating rather than a set of culinary precepts that characterizes contemporary cookery. The best professional cooks have been well trained in the basics of traditional cuisine, but they don't feel bound by ironclad rules. Classic *beurre blanc* and hollandaise sauces, for example, are much used today but they may be lightened by the addition of fresh herbs or piquant sorrel.

Modern agricultural and distribution techniques have given us access to every conceivable kind of food, while unprecedented affluence permits an increasing percentage of disposable income to be spent on food in wealthy countries. Technologically superb kitchen equipment such as electric pasta makers, ice-cream makers, and, especially, food processors, enable home cooks to prepare meals as sophisticated as those eaten in restaurants. Pâtés and mousses, for example, used to be turned out primarily by professional kitchens; today anyone with a food processor can whip up an airy creation such as the Cold Salmon Mousse with Sour Cream–Romaine Dressing or the Scallop Terrine with Scallion Sauce found in this book.

Health concerns, perhaps more than anything else, have prompted us to change our eating habits. In recent years the human diet has been subjected to intense scrutiny by medical science, whose general conclusion is that if we ate more like peasants we would feel more like kings. The average American diet is too high in meat and animal fats, too high in sugars, too low in complex carbohydrates (beans, rice, wheat, corn), and too low in fruits and vegetables. Virtually all major health organizations agree that our rich, high-fat, low-fiber diet is responsible for unprecedented levels of heart disease, hypertension, certain cancers, obesity, and adult onset diabetes. We've been urged to return to a diet resembling in many ways the one our ancestors used to eat and, while we're at it, to lead the kind of active life they did.

We are not, of course, going to eat like true peasants any more than we'll go out and work in the fields with hand plows. We're more inclined to get our excercise through recreation. And we'll eat high-carbohydrate pasta, but we'll liven it up with shrimp and fresh ginger.

We'll serve beans, but they may be garnished with sun-dried tomatoes. We'll borrow guacamole from Mexican cooking to top New England's crab cakes, and we'll lace traditional British Christmas pudding with America's fresh cranberries.

Since the recipes in this book are mostly straightforward and simple, without the complicated sauces and technical tours de force required of haute cuisine, even beginning cooks should have little trouble following most of them. In view of the fact that few of us today have the time or inclination to spend hours in the kitchen, I'm offering recipes that may be quickly prepared and quickly cooked. A section of suggested menus is included in the book to help guide the way toward foolproof entertaining.

My own feeling is that the spirit of peasant cookery lies in preparing nourishing, imaginative, and fresh-tasting meals for family and friends rather than dazzling others with culinary brilliance. Culinary elegance is characterized by simplicity and freshness, by attractive presentation. The most successful evenings occur when guests and hosts alike are not just well fed, but relaxed and enjoying the company. Or, as Gilbert and Sullivan put it, "It isn't so much what's on the table that counts, as what's on the chairs."

SOME NOTES ON INGREDIENTS

Most of the ingredients called for in these recipes are available in any market. The less common items can usually be found in major metropolitan areas, and even the more "exotic" foods are showing up in rural and suburban places as well, as increasingly sophisticated consumers urge their markets to carry a wider variety of products.

Some produce, such as red-leafed radicchio, arugula, Belgian endive, and mâche (or corn salad), is still hard to find in many parts of the United States, but home gardeners can order seeds for these tasty salad greens from almost any seed company. I know people who grow radicchio and arugula in their city window boxes, and I myself have grown delicate leaf lettuces there.

Many of the recipes call for goat cheese, or chèvre as it's called in French. Chèvre comes hard or soft, mild or sharp-flavored. It is an excellent cheese for today's diet since it is lower in fat and calories than many cow's-milk cheeses. In several of the recipes I've suggested using a creamy chèvre such as Montrachet, a regularly imported French cheese, but there is an ever-increasing supply of domestic goat cheeses being made in communities all over the United States that could be used just as well.

Wild mushrooms (many of them now raised commercially) are also becoming widely available in American markets. Shiitake mushrooms are perhaps the best known of these. Used only in Japan until a few years ago, these flavorful fungi are now available fresh in many supermarkets. I don't think there's any harm in substituting one wild mushroom for another in most cases. In the recipe for Mâche with Warm Shiitake Mushrooms, for example, I've used chanterelles when they were available; the flavor is different but equally delicious.

Crème fraîche, that refreshing, lightly soured cream used in French cooking, can now be bought in many shops that specialize in imported cheeses, or you can make your own according to the recipe in this book.

Certain other ingredients, such as tahini (sesame paste) and Chinese black bean sauce, can usually be found in grocery stores that carry Middle Eastern and Oriental products, or in health-food stores.

Fresh herbs, the hallmark of contemporary cooking, have become increasingly available from greengrocers in the past year or two. They are still somewhat seasonal; sorrel, for example, is almost impossible to find except in spring and summer (it comes along, happily enough, just when the shad are running so that Shad Roe with Sorrel Hollandaise is a perfectly timed combination). At nurseries I've sometimes found little pots of herbs that grocery stores seldom carry fresh, such as sage. Incidentally, I try to keep a window box filled with herbs growing all year, bringing it indoors for the winter.

Many mail-order distributors carry a variety of hard-to-find ingredients, ranging from hot peppers to blue cornmeal to mushroom spores (so that you can grow your own). I have not included a list of these companies because my experience has been that they come and go at a rapid rate. But they're well worth scouting out, particularly if you live in an area that is undersupplied with imaginative ingredients.

APPETIZERS, HORS D'OEUVRES, AND FIRST COURSES

You help yourself to caviar, with lemon juice if you prefer it that way, then you have a radish with salt, and another piece of herring . . .

Chekov

A festive Russian meal that didn't begin with hors d'oeuvres, or *zakuski,* would be like plunging straight into the vigorous main portion of Tchaikovsky's *Romeo and Juliet* without being led up to it by the slow introductory passage. The Russian gentry elevated *zakuski* (or *zaiedki,* the older, more rustic word) to a glorious and extravagant level, but the custom of serving something to nibble on with pre-dinner glasses of vodka originated with the Russian peasantry. Simple marinated mushrooms, pickles, or slivers of salted fish were the kind of thing they served, and of course, whenever it was affordable, caviar.

Italian peasants rarely ate the elaborate antipasti—literally "before the meal"—served in restaurants and at formal dinners. Sweet fresh figs or fragrant melon slices with a thin slice of *prosciutto* or *salame* was a more typical way to begin a festive peasant meal in Italy. A Greek peasant would nibble on a piece of feta cheese or a bit of *tarama* (fish roe) along with his glass of wine or ouzo over ice, while his Chinese counterpart might dig into a selection of "little dishes" to begin a celebratory meal: Mongolian fried peanuts, tangy Hunan pickles, or spiced and crunchy soybeans.

A true French peasant would no more think of diving into a meal without a preliminary hors d'oeuvres—a few olives or crisp radishes, say—than he would venture out on a winter's day without a beret to protect his head. In Japanese restaurants the well-to-do began their dinners with a lavish and elegant assortment of *zensai,* but in simpler homes lilliputian portions of pickled eggplant or turnip, lotus root, or ginko nuts might be offered.

The common characteristic of peasant appetizers is that their emphasis is on stimulating the appetite, not dulling it. Spicy flavors and pickled foods. Salty-smoky fish and fish roe. The fresh flavors of raw fruits and vegetables. Crunchy textures. These are the qualities of peasant hors d'oeuvres that work so well to get the gustatory juices flowing. Too much high-fat cheese, heavy dips and rich pâtés, on the other hand, numb the stomach and overload the taste buds.

We are fortunate today to have access to many ingredients that enable us to incorporate some of the best peasant traditions into our own appetizers. Chinese fermented black beans, for example, add piquancy to mushroom pâté. Goat cheese, which is lower in fat and calories than many other cheeses, is now available in many forms, either foreign or domestic, throughout the United States. Lumpfish roe, sold in small jars at reasonable prices, has long been an acceptable substitute for caviar in certain preparations.

Whether nibbling on hors d'oeuvres in the living room with drinks before dinner, or sitting down at the table to an introductory first course, the appetite will best be awakened by food that is attractively presented (after all, visual pleasure is an important part of gustatory satisfaction), that has interesting texture and assertive flavor to stimulate the palate, and that provides just enough nourishment to soothe hunger pangs and absorb liquor.

At a Scandinavian peasant wedding, guests help themselves to thin slices of salt-cured meat, lift their glasses of aquavit, and toast *"skoal."* *"A votre santé,"* murmurs a French fisherman, tipping his glass of *pastis* toward his companions and helping himself to another fresh-grilled sardine. *"Salud"*: the Spaniard drains his glass of sherry and reaches toward the selection of *tapas* for a handful of tiny briny shrimp. In

Poland a farmer's wife passes a plate of hot meat and cabbage pasties to the assembled guests while her husband raises his glass of vodka and proposes, "*Na zdrowie.*"
Cheers!

Quesadillas with Leeks and Goat Cheese

Mushroom Pâté with Black Bean Sauce

Eggplant Caviar with Caviar

Garlic-Basil Shortbreads

Mushroom-filled Blue Cornmeal Turnovers

Chicken Liver-Apple Terrine

Turnip Canapés with Chicken and Chutney

Eggplant with Goat Cheese and Walnuts

Cornmeal Crêpes with Crème Fraîche and Caviar

Broiled Mushrooms Stuffed with Goat Cheese

Vegetable Pâté with Green Mayonnaise

Walnut-Garlic Dip

White Bean Dip

QUESADILLAS WITH LEEKS AND GOAT CHEESE

Quesadillas are Mexican turnovers that are usually filled with simple cheese-based mixtures. This recipe adds a European twist with goat cheese. The result is an exceptionally savory and simple-to-make first course that would enhance any meal. Follow it with Salmon with Soy Sauce and Lime, for example, or Chicken with Fresh Figs, Port, and Basil, and serve Chocolate Pudding with Praline for dessert.

Serves 6

1 bunch leeks (about 3 medium leeks)
1 tablespoon (15 ml) oil
2 medium cloves garlic, minced

6 ounces (168 g) soft goat cheese, such as Montrachet
6 flour tortillas
Oil

Trim the leeks and cut them in half lengthwise. Rinse carefully to eliminate all sand and grit. Cut them in 4-inch (100-mm) lengths. Cook leeks with 1 tablespoon (15 ml) oil and garlic over low heat in a covered skillet about 40 minutes, or until they are very soft. Turn occasionally during cooking to prevent scorching.

Spread cheese over half of each tortilla. Divide the leeks among them. Fold tortillas in half and arrange them on a baking sheet. Brush the top surface with a little oil. Bake in a 400°F. oven about 6 to 8 minutes, or until filling is hot and tortillas are crisp and lightly browned.

MUSHROOM PÂTÉ with BLACK BEAN SAUCE

Chinese peasants have been flavoring their food with black bean sauce (available in stores that carry Oriental foods) for centuries. For some reason, when the black bean sauce is combined with mushrooms in this dish the result looks and tastes a bit like traditional meat pâté.

Serve with toast or crackers. This pâté begs to be taken on a picnic!

Serves 4 to 6

½ pound (225 g) mushrooms, sliced
2 medium shallots, or 1 small onion, chopped
1 tablespoon (15 ml) lemon juice

1 tablespoon (15 ml) oil
2 tablespoons (30 ml) sweet butter
3 to 4 tablespoons (45 to 60 ml) black bean sauce

Cook mushrooms, shallots, and lemon juice in oil and butter over very low heat for about 10 minutes, stirring frequently, until mushrooms are very soft but not too brown. Transfer mixture to food processor or blender and pulverize it. Place in a small decorative bowl, loaf pan, terrine, or pâté mold. Stir in black bean sauce to taste—some brands are much saltier than others. Pack mixture down with a spatula or spoon. Cover and refrigerate several hours or overnight. Serve directly from the bowl or terrine.

ADVANCE PREPARATION: May be made 1 or 2 days in advance.

EGGPLANT CAVIAR with CAVIAR

Peasants from the Balkan states are credited with the invention of a caviar substitute made from eggplant. Called variously poor man's caviar or eggplant caviar, this traditional hors d'oeuvre undergoes a happy transformation with a little of the real thing sprinkled over it.

Serves 8 to 10

1 medium eggplant, about 1¼ to 1½ pounds (562 to 675 g)	Dash red pepper flakes
	1 tablespoon (15 ml) lemon juice
½ cup (125 ml) olive oil	Salt
1 to 2 large cloves garlic, minced	Pepper

GARNISH:

2 Belgian endives	Lemon wedges
2 tablespoons (30 ml) black lumpfish roe or caviar	

Cut stem ends off eggplant. Cut eggplant in half lengthwise and rub cut sides with a little of the oil. Place eggplant halves, cut side down, on a baking sheet. Bake at 425°F. for about 30 minutes, or until eggplant is very soft.

Cut cooked unpeeled eggplant in 1-inch (25-mm) pieces and place them in the blender or food processor. With the machine running, add the garlic and pepper flakes. Drizzle in the oil in a steady stream. Add lemon juice, salt, and pepper. Turn machine off and taste mixture for seasoning.

Separate the leaves from the endives. Spread each leaf with some of the eggplant mixture and sprinkle a little caviar over it. Arrange on a serving platter garnished with lemon wedges.

ADVANCE PREPARATION: The eggplant mixture may be made up to 3 days in advance and refrigerated. The endive leaves may be garnished an hour or two before serving, but the caviar should go on at the last minute.

GARLIC-BASIL SHORTBREADS

Garlic is a traditional appetite-enhancer. In Spain you might start a meal with sopa de ajo, *or garlic soup, and in Italy you would dip vegetables in garlicky* bagna cauda. *Romanians eat* mititei—*garlic sausages—as a prelude to a meal, while in Provence,* tapénade *is one of the many garlic-infused appetizers. True to form, these crunchy shortbreads quicken the appetite. Serve them with drinks before dinner.*

Rice flour or cornstarch is often added to shortbread because each adds a delicate, almost silky texture. Buy rice flour at a health food store or in any store where Oriental food products are sold.

Yields 16

1 cup (250 ml) unbleached flour	1 tablespoon (15 ml) oil
½ cup (125 ml) rice flour or cornstarch	Salt
	3 medium cloves garlic, minced
5 tablespoons (75 ml) butter, cut in 5 pieces	¼ cup (60 ml) minced fresh basil, or 1 teaspoon (5 ml) dried
¼ cup (60 ml) white wine	
1 egg yolk	

Place flour, rice flour or cornstarch, and butter in food processor. Turn machine on and off three or four times, until mixture has the consistency of coarse meal.

Whisk together wine, egg yolk, oil, salt, and garlic. Stir in basil. With machine running, pour liquid mixture in a steady stream into the flour mixture. Turn machine off immediately.

Press dough into the bottom of a buttered 9-inch (225-mm) pie pan or cake pan. Crimp the edges with a fork. Mark into 16 wedges with a knife. If possible, refrigerate for 30 minutes.

Preheat oven to 400°F. Bake the shortbread for 5 minutes, then turn oven down to 350°F. and continue baking for another 30 minutes, or until shortbread is beginning to color lightly. Let cool before cutting through the wedges.

MUSHROOM-FILLED BLUE CORNMEAL TURNOVERS

Small individual pastries filled with such things as meat, mushrooms, rice, or vegetables have been emerging from peasant kitchens since cooking began. Consider Russian pirozhki, Chinese pork dumplings, Latin American empanadas, and Cornish pastries.

I first tasted blue cornmeal tortillas at the Second Mesa during a trip to the Southwest many years ago. The delicate blue color and subtle flavor seemed quite magical to me at the time, and indeed, blue cornmeal is considered by Native Americans to have special spiritual significance. Many stores specializing in imported and "gourmet" foods now sell blue cornmeal, as do a few specialty mail-order catalogs. It can be used in pancakes, waffles, breads, and muffins.

Makes about 30 turnovers

FILLING:

1 small shallot

5 to 6 medium mushrooms, about 4 ounces (112 g) total

1 tablespoon (15 ml) sweet butter

PASTRY:

1½ cups (375 ml) flour

½ cup (125 ml) blue cornmeal

Salt

½ cup (125 ml) sweet butter

¼ cup (60 ml) cold water

1 egg yolk

1 tablespoon (15 ml) cold water

For the filling, mince shallot and mushrooms finely and cook them in butter over medium-low heat about 5 minutes, or until shallots are soft and translucent. If necessary, raise heat and continue cooking until all juices have evaporated. Remove from heat and let cool.

For the pastry, blend flour, cornmeal, salt, and butter together until mixture resembles coarse meal (may be done in food processor). Add enough cold water so that dough holds together and may be formed into a ball.

Roll dough out into a thin sheet, about ⅛ inch (3 mm) thick. With a cookie cutter or a small drinking glass (about 2½-inch [62-mm] diameter), cut the dough into circles. Place a spoonful of the cooled mushroom filling on one-half of each circle. Fold the other half over it, pressing the edges together and crimping them with a fork (sometimes they balk at sticking together properly; if this happens, moisten one edge with a very small amount of water).

Preheat the oven to 400°F.

Arrange the turnovers on one or two baking sheets. Beat the egg yolk with 1 tablespoon (15 ml) cold water and brush the top of the turnovers with this mixture. Bake in a preheated 400°F. oven for 25 to 30 minutes, or until turnovers are lightly browned.

ADVANCE PREPARATION: May be made a few hours in advance, refrigerated, and baked just before serving. Or make up to 2 or 3 weeks ahead of time and freeze the unbaked turnovers; bake just before serving.

CHICKEN LIVER-APPLE TERRINE

The word terrine *originally referred to the sturdy earthenware dish that many French peasant preparations were baked in, but it has now come to refer to almost any kind of pâté. Serve this fresh-tasting hors d'oeuvre on toast points or crackers.*

Serves 4 to 6

1 medium shallot, minced
1 medium apple, peeled, cored, and coarsely chopped
2 tablespoons (30 ml) sweet butter
¼ pound (112 g) chicken livers
1 small pinch nutmeg
Salt
¼ teaspoon (1.5 ml) thyme
4 tablespoons (60 ml) Calvados or brandy
¼ cup (60 ml) water
½ package (about 1 teaspoon [5 ml]) gelatin

Cook shallot and apple in butter until apple is soft. Add the livers and cook until they are barely pink in the center. Stir in nutmeg, salt, and thyme. Transfer mixture to a food processor, but do not wash skillet. Add 2 tablespoons (30 ml) of the Calvados or brandy to the livers and purée until mixture is well blended but still has a little texture. Transfer to a small decorative terrine or serving bowl.

Add ¼ cup (60 ml) water to the skillet and heat it, stirring up browned bits. Turn off heat and sprinkle in the gelatin, stirring until it is dissolved. Stir in remaining 2 tablespoons (30 ml) Calvados or brandy and pour liquid mixture over the top of the chicken liver mixture.

Refrigerate several hours or overnight.

ADVANCE PREPARATION: May be made a day or two in advance.

TURNIP CANAPÉS WITH CHICKEN AND CHUTNEY

Turnips and other root vegetables—carrots, leeks, onions, and radishes— kept the European peasantry alive through many lean periods. We usually encounter this humble vegetable cooked to a fare-thee-well in stews and soups, but the fine peppery flavor and satisfactory crunch of sliced raw turnips make them an ideal low-calorie base for canapés.

Makes 20 to 25 canapés

1 small boneless chicken breast
1 bay leaf
½ teaspoon (3 ml) dried tarragon
1 medium onion, minced
2 tablespoons (30 ml) sweet butter
1 pinch nutmeg
⅛ teaspoon (.5 ml) cayenne pepper
2 tablespoons (30 ml) mango chutney
3 small turnips
2 tablespoons (30 ml) minced parsley

Place chicken breast in a saucepan and cover with water. Add bay leaf and tarragon and simmer about 15 minutes, or until chicken is cooked clear through. Remove chicken, reserving broth. When cool enough to handle, chop chicken coarsely.

Cook onion in butter until limp and translucent. Place in food processor along with chicken, nutmeg, and cayenne. Add 3 tablespoons (45 ml) of the chicken broth and process until mixture is smooth. Add chutney and turn machine on and off quickly two or three times, so that chutney is chopped but not puréed.

Scrub turnips and cut in slices about ⅛ inch (3 mm) thick. Spread each with chicken mixture, garnish with parsley, and arrange on a serving dish.

EGGPLANT WITH
GOAT CHEESE AND WALNUTS

Every peasant who owns a goat ends up sooner or later with goat cheese, or chèvre. There are dozens of different kinds of chèvre: soft and creamy or cheddar-hard, strong-flavored or mild, domestic or imported—something for every palate. For this recipe, use a creamy one, such as French Montrachet.

Serve this as a spread for crackers or a dip for vegetables. It can also be used to make a simple lunch: spread it on pieces of French bread or English muffins, toast until hot and bubbly, and serve with a green salad.

Serves 6 to 8

1 cup (250 ml) chopped eggplant (unpeeled)
2 tablespoons (30 ml) plus ½ cup (125 ml) olive oil
2 tablespoons (30 ml) chopped parsley
½ teaspoon (3 ml) red pepper flakes, or a few drops Tabasco

3 cloves garlic, coarsley chopped
½ cup (125 ml) coarsely chopped walnuts
3 ounces (84 g) soft goat cheese
Salt

Toss the eggplant with 2 tablespoons (30 ml) oil. Bake in a 450°F. oven about 30 minutes, stirring occasionally, until soft and browned (may be done in a toaster oven). Transfer to a food processor or blender. Add parsley. With the motor running, drop in the pepper flakes and garlic. Pour in the remaining ½ cup (125 ml) olive oil, then add the walnuts. Continue to process another second or two, until mixture is thick. Transfer to a bowl and add the goat cheese, stirring until well blended. Stir in salt to taste.

ADVANCE PREPARATION: May be made up to a day in advance.

CORNMEAL CRÊPES WITH
CRÈME FRAÎCHE AND CAVIAR

Restaurants from Paris to Los Angeles are serving delicate cornmeal crêpes these days. They are part Mexican corn tortilla, part Jewish blintz, with a hint of American pancake and Russian blini thrown in. These are truly cross-cultural crêpes!

If the crêpes are made ahead of time this is an easy first course to assemble at the last minute. Use real caviar if you're so inclined, but less expensive black lumpfish roe is perfectly acceptable here.

Serves 6

CRÊPES:

1 cup (250 ml) milk
1 cup (250 ml) water
4 eggs
3 tablespoons (45 ml) melted butter
1½ cups (375 ml) flour
½ cup (125 ml) cornmeal
Salt
1 cup (250 ml) Crème Fraîche (recipe follows)
3 ounces (84 g) caviar or black lumpfish roe

GARNISH:
Lemon wedges

Combine all ingredients for the crêpes. Cook them in a lightly oiled crêpe pan or small skillet over medium heat for a few seconds on each side, until very lightly browned (adjust heat as necessary).

To serve, place a spoonful of Crème Fraîche on each crêpe. Sprinkle a little caviar over it and fold crêpe in half. Arrange three or four crêpes on each of six serving plates. Garnish each with a lemon wedge.

ADVANCE PREPARATION: Crêpes may be cooked up to 2 or 3 days in advance and refrigerated. Or make them a week or two in advance and freeze. To serve, wrap crêpes in foil and place in a low oven for about 30 minutes, or until they are warm.

CRÈME FRAÎCHE

1 cup (250 ml) whipping cream, preferably not ultrapasteurized
2 tablespoons (30 ml) buttermilk or yogurt

Stir cream and buttermilk or yogurt together in a glass or ceramic bowl or jar. Cover and let stand at room temperature until mixture is about as thick as sour cream; this will take from 12 to 24 hours, depending on temperature. Refrigerate as soon as it has thickened. Will keep for up to a week.

BROILED MUSHROOMS
STUFFED with GOAT CHEESE

When the cultivated mushroom Agaricus bisporus *was developed in France in the eighteenth century, it was a luxury only the rich could afford; peasants picked wild mushrooms in the fields and woods. Today wild mushrooms are becoming scarce as development squeezes out the countryside. Ironically, they are now farmed and sold in markets for such high prices that cultivated mushrooms are a bargain by comparison.*

To make predinner finger-food appetizers, use small, bite-sized mushrooms. For a first course or side dish to accompany meat dishes, select larger mushrooms.

Serves 6 to 8

About 24 small cultivated mushrooms, or 12 large
1 medium shallot, finely minced

2 teaspoons (10 ml) oil
3 ounces (84 g) soft goat cheese (such as Montrachet)

Rinse and pat mushrooms dry. Separate stems from caps. Mince the stems. Cook the shallots and mushroom stems in oil until soft. Transfer mixture to a bowl and blend with the goat cheese. Fill mushroom caps with this mixture.

About 20 minutes before serving, preheat the broiler. Broil mushrooms about 8 to 10 minutes, or until hot and bubbly (may be done in toaster oven).

ADVANCE PREPARATION: Mushrooms may be stuffed up to a day ahead of time and refrigerated, covered, until just before broiling.

VEGETABLE PÂTÉ with
GREEN MAYONNAISE

Vegetable mousses and pâtés are popular today because they are nonfattening and light-tasting. When I was a child, I used to spend weekends with a friend on her grandmother's farm outside Paris, where one of the things we were given to eat was a sort of cold vegetable soufflé. It may even have been leftovers from the night before, but in any event it seemed delicious at the time, and I think of it as the forerunner of today's vegetable pâtés.

I've used canned white beans successfully in this recipe, but for really deep flavor try making the White Bean Dip and using that. Serve this as a first course at a summer dinner, followed by Scallops with Braised Fennel and Fresh Tomato Tart.

Serves 6 to 8

VEGETABLE PÂTÉ:

2 cups (500 ml) cooked white beans
1 tablespoon (15 ml) gelatin
¼ cup (60 ml) warm water
Salt
¼ teaspoon (1.5 ml) cayenne pepper
3 medium carrots, peeled and cut in strips about 3 inches (75 mm) long

¼ pound (112 g) green beans
¼ pound (112 g) mushrooms
1 tablespoon (15 ml) butter
Mayonnaise with Fresh Herbs (recipe follows)

Purée beans in a blender or food processor. Dissolve gelatin in ¼ cup (60 ml) warm water. With motor running, pour gelatin into beans in a steady stream. Add salt and cayenne. Scrape mixture into a bowl and reserve.

Cook carrots and green beans separately in simmering water (or steam them) until tender—about 5 minutes for the carrots, 10 for the beans. Keeping them separate, chop the vegetables coarsely.

Slice the mushrooms and cook them in 1 tablespoon (15 ml) butter about 3 minutes over medium-high heat.

Oil bottom and sides of a 6–cup (1500-ml) loaf pan. Spread a layer of bean purée about an inch (25 mm) thick on bottom of mold. Spread the chopped carrots on top of this, followed by a thin layer of bean purée. Spread the chopped green beans over this, add another layer of puréed beans, then the mushrooms, and finally, the remaining bean purée. Refrigerate the pâté several hours or overnight.

To serve, unmold pâté and cut in slices. Pass a bowl of Mayonnaise with Fresh Herbs separately.

MAYONNAISE WITH FRESH HERBS

Yields 2½ to 3 cups

1 cup (250 ml) watercress
1 cup (250 ml) parsley
2 tablespoons (30 ml) chopped chives or green onions
1 cup (250 ml) mayonnaise (preferably homemade)

1 cup (250 ml) yogurt
2 tablespoons (30 ml) lemon juice
2 tablespoons (30 ml) capers

Mince watercress, parsley, and chives or green onions finely with a knife or in food processor. Combine with remaining ingredients. Serve with vegetable or seafood pâtés and mousses, or as a dip for raw vegetables.

WALNUT-GARLIC DIP

There was a time when the upper classes shunned garlic, associating it with the peasantry. Too bad for them—they missed out on this pungent dip. Serve an assortment of crisp raw vegetables with it: sliced jícama, red pepper strips, whole snow peas, endive leaves, halved brussels sprouts, etc. If you're lucky enough to have any of the dip left over, dab it on fish or chicken before grilling, or stir it into oil and vinegar for a salad.

Yields about 1½ cups

1 cup (250 ml) walnut halves
3 to 4 medium cloves garlic
⅓ cup (85 ml) olive oil

Salt
1 to 2 tablespoons (15 to 30 ml) hot water

Blend all ingredients, except the hot water in a food processor or blender. Add a tablespoon or two (15 to 30 ml) of hot water to thin mixture to proper consistency.

WHITE BEAN DIP

Mashed dried peas or beans, usually meant to be scooped up with bread or pita, are a staple in many different cultures. One of the best known of these is Middle Eastern hummus made from chick peas. In rural France, white beans mashed with garlic and oil is called Brandade à la Soissonaise. *Serve this with triangles of pita bread, crackers, or a selection of raw vegetables.*

Serves 6 to 8

2 cups (500 ml) cooked white beans

3 tablespoons (45 ml) lemon juice

¼ cup (60 ml) olive oil

2 tablespoons (30 ml) tahini (sesame paste), optional

2 large cloves garlic, minced

Salt

Cayenne pepper

Purée all ingredients in a blender or food processor.

SOUPS

Soup of the evening, beautiful soup!

Lewis Carroll

What could be more representative of the peasant kitchen than a pot of soup bubbling on the back of the stove? Warming, soothing, filling, nourishing, inexpensive, and simple to make, soups have kept the world's peasantry alive since cooking began. The broth from a pot-au-feu greeted the French *paysan* coming in from the fields, cool borscht revived Russian and Polish laborers on blistering summer days. Native Americans made a favorite soup by dropping scalding stones into baskets of water and acorns. Africans are partial to peanut soup, the Japanese may eat soup at breakfast, lunch, and dinner, and the Chinese serve light soups throughout the course of a banquet. There are hundreds, probably thousands, of different soups in the world, including cream soups and broths, bean soups and cold jellied bouillon, chowders, bisques, and potages.

Contemporary soups tend to be lighter and fresher than the constantly brewing stockpot type that nourished our ancestors. Few of us have the time to monitor an all-day simmering kettle of soup, nor are our taste buds enthusiastic about overcooked vegetables. And we have mostly tired of the heavy, predictable taste of canned soups that did so much to liberate our mothers from the stove during the mid-twentieth century. Technology has adapted to contemporary tastes or, more likely, vice versa. We now demand the freshest possible ingredients, which are available year-round, and thanks to high-speed blenders and food processors, the work of chopping and puréeing ingredients is accomplished in a flash. The result is quickly prepared, smooth, and very fresh soups that require only a few minutes' cooking time.

The availability of good canned tomatoes, chicken broth, and beef broth makes the task of creating homemade soups even simpler. I recommend checking the list of ingredients on canned broths, however: some list simple, basic ingredients while others contain a variety of additives and colorings that do nothing for flavor. I've not yet found dried soups or bouillon cubes that don't contain a long list of artificial ingredients, therefore I choose not to use them. Of course, fresh *anything* is probably better than canned, so if you have the time and inclination, by all means make your own stocks (many people freeze stock in ice-cube trays and store the cubes in freezer bags for quick and convenient use).

Peasant soups are quite often hearty meal-in-a-bowl affairs that are not meant to be followed by a substantial main course. Bouillabaisse, minestrone, split pea with ham, onion soup gratiné, are all filling soups that should be a meal in themselves (along with bread and a salad) or be followed by light dishes: broiled meats or fish, simple pasta, or a vegetable dish such as Zucchini Tian with Goat Cheese. With a more substantial main course, keep the soups light and refreshing. Most of the soups in this section are designed to be served as a first course for almost any meal.

*Cream of White Bean Soup with Roasted
Red Pepper Rouille*

Eggplant-Garlic Soup

Corn Chowder with Tarragon

Broccoli-Fennel Soup

Rutabaga-Tomato Soup

Arugula Soup

Crab Chowder with Crème Fraîche and Lime

Beet Broth with Sour Cream

Butternut Soup with Orange Crème Fraîche

Chilled Avocado Soup with Buttermilk

Cold Carrot Soup with Guacamole

See also:

Tortellini in Brodo with Swiss Chard and Red Pepper

CREAM OF WHITE BEAN SOUP WITH ROASTED RED PEPPER ROUILLE

Dried beans and other legumes have been a mainstay of the human diet at least as far back as the ancient Sumerians. Egyptians ate them and so did ancient Mexican civilizations. Puréed dried beans were standard fare for most medieval Europeans, who could afford little else. Fortunately for the outcome of civilization, dried beans are among the most nutritious of foods, providing protein, vitamins, and fiber, as well as being fat-free and low in calories.

Rouille, that heady sauce traditionally used to bring out the flavors of bouillabaisse and other French fish soups, also adds invigorating flavor and a splash of color to bean soup. It may be put to many other good uses as well: toss it with pasta, or spoon it over fried eggs, boiled potatoes or cauliflower, or broiled fish. Spread it on bread and you've got a glorified version of the standard Provençal peasant breakfast (bread, olive oil, and garlic).

Serves 6

CREAM OF WHITE BEAN SOUP:

- 1 onion, minced
- 3 cloves garlic, minced
- 1 tablespoon (15 ml) butter
- 4 cups (1000 ml) cooked white beans (such as navy or cannellini beans)
- 6 cups (1500 ml) chicken stock
- Salt

OPTIONAL GARNISH:
   Roasted Red Pepper
   Rouille (recipe follows)

   Cook the onion and garlic in the butter over medium–low heat until onions are soft. Add the beans and chicken stock. Simmer 15 minutes. Add salt. Purée mixture, in batches, in a blender or food processor.
   To serve, ladle soup into individual bowls and top each with a small spoonful of rouille. Pass remaining rouille separately.

ADVANCE PREPARATION: Soup may be made 1 or 2 days in advance.

ROASTED RED PEPPER ROUILLE
   1 medium red bell pepper
   1 small fresh hot red pepper,
      or 1 teaspoon (5 ml) dried
      red pepper flakes, or
      few drops Tabasco
   3 large cloves garlic, minced

   ½ cup (125 ml) bread
      crumbs
      Salt
   ¾ cup (180 ml) olive oil
   1 egg yolk (optional, see
      Note)

   Cut bell pepper in quarters, remove seeds and membrane, and broil, skin side up, until black and blistered (may be done in a toaster oven). Peel off skin and place pepper in a food processor or blender. Mince hot pepper finely and add it (or pepper flakes or Tabasco) to the bell pepper. Add garlic, bread crumbs, and salt. With machine running, slowly drizzle in olive oil.

NOTE: If mixture fails to thicken, or if you want a creamier sauce, place a raw egg yolk in the food processor or blender and drizzle the rouille into it with the machine running.

ADVANCE PREPARATION: May be made up to 2 days in advance and refrigerated. Whisk with a fork if mixture separates.

EGGPLANT-GARLIC SOUP

The only eggplant most of us know is the large, deep-purple variety sold in most markets. But the small, elongated eggplants that are much better for grilling or sautéing are becoming more popular, and many home gardeners are growing the shiny white ones available from seed companies. Although we don't use eggplants much in American cooking, they are a staple in Mediterranean and Balkan peasant kitchens.

This is a good soup to set the stage for a dinner party. To give it a good, rustic Provençal flavor, pass a bowl of Roasted Red Pepper Rouille or Aïoli along with it.

Serves 6

4 small eggplants, or 1 large, about 1¼ pounds (562 g) total
1 medium onion, minced
¼ cup (60 ml) olive oil

8 whole medium cloves garlic, peeled
5 cups (1250 ml) water
Salt

OPTIONAL GARNISH:
Roasted Red Pepper Rouille (see Cream of White Bean Soup) or Aïoli (recipe follows)

Trim off ends, but do not peel eggplant. Cut into 2-inch (50-mm) pieces. Cook eggplant and onion in olive oil over medium heat, stirring frequently, until eggplant begins to brown and soften. Stir in garlic cloves and cook another 2 minutes. Add water and salt and simmer, uncovered, about 30 minutes, or until eggplant is very tender. Purée mixture in food processor or blender in two or three batches.

ADVANCE PREPARATION: Soup may be made a day or two in advance.

AÏOLI

Traditional aïoli is made by pounding all the ingredients together with a mortar and pestle. Although some people feel that garlic takes on a bitter quality from being pulverized in a blender or food processor, the following preparation is expedient and satisfactory for most purposes.

Yields about 1 cup

1 egg yolk
4 to 6 medium cloves garlic, minced
1 cup (250 ml) olive oil

Salt
1 tablespoon (15 ml) lemon juice

Place the egg yolk in a blender or food processor. Stir the garlic into the olive oil. With the machine running, pour oil into the blender, drop by drop at first, then in a steady stream, until mixture emulsifies. Add salt and lemon juice.

CORN CHOWDER WITH TARRAGON

Though a native of the New World, corn became a staple in peasant recipes in such disparate places as Spain, Italy, Africa, and the Balkans. The original corn soup was a Native American dish with no butter, milk, or cream in it—European settlers contributed these ingredients.

Serve this soup as a first course, or make a meal of it in late summer when corn is at its peak, accompanied by a big platter of Tomatoes with Balsamic Vinegar and Shallots.

Serves 4 to 6

6 to 8 ears corn
3 tablespoons (45 ml) butter
1 small onion, minced
4 cups (1000 ml) milk
Salt

1 tablespoon (15 ml) minced fresh tarragon, or 1 teaspoon (5 ml) dried
½ cup (125 ml) half-and-half

Holding each ear of corn over a bowl to catch milky juices, cut kernels off ears with a sharp knife (yield should be about 1½ to 2 cups [375 to 500 ml] kernels).

Melt butter over medium-low heat and stir in onion. Continue cooking, stirring occasionally, until onion is translucent. Add corn and all accumulated juices, milk, salt, tarragon, and half-and-half. Simmer about 5 to 8 minutes.

BROCCOLI-FENNEL SOUP

Broccoli has been one of Italy's favorite vegetables for centuries. It was introduced to America as early as 1720 but never really caught on until the 1920s. Proof once again how strange and often inexplicable food tastes are: we accepted cabbage and cauliflower cheerfully, but turned up our noses at their close cousin broccoli (all are members of the mustard or cruciferous family).

This simple soup makes a good introduction to any meal. The vegetables give it a good earthy flavor, but since it has neither cream nor butter, appetites won't be overwhelmed.

Serves 6 to 8

1 pound (450 g) potatoes (3 to 4 medium potatoes)

2 quarts (2000 ml) water or chicken stock

1 bunch broccoli, about 1½ pounds (675 g)

1 fennel bulb

Salt

Pepper

Peel potatoes and cut in quarters. Place them in a kettle with water or chicken stock. Simmer about 10 minutes, or until tender.

Cut the broccoli into large chunks, peeling the stalks if they are tough. Chop the fennel coarsely. Add broccoli and fennel to the potatoes and continue simmering until all the vegetables are tender, about 20 minutes.

Purée the soup in a food processor or blender, in several batches if necessary. Salt and pepper to taste and reheat if necessary. Serve hot or chilled.

ADVANCE PREPARATION: May be made the day before serving.

RUTABAGA-TOMATO SOUP

Rutabagas are large yellow turnips and, like most root vegetables, they are frequently used in peasant soups and stews. Sometimes called "Swedish turnips," rutabagas are associated with Scandinavian cuisine and were therefore a staple in Swedish-influenced midwestern American cooking. The rutabaga adds vivid color and piquant flavor to ordinary tomato soup.

Store-bought rutabagas must be peeled since they are coated with thick wax.

Serves 6 to 8

1 large rutabaga

3 to 4 large fresh tomatoes, or 15 ounces (420 g) canned

2 cups (500 ml) chicken stock

Salt

OPTIONAL GARNISH:

1 cup (250 ml) Crème
 Fraîche (see Cornmeal
 Crêpes with Crème
 Fraîche and Caviar for
 recipe) or whipped cream

1 tablespoon (15 ml) finely
 minced arugula or
 watercress leaves

Peel rutabaga and cut in chunks. Place it in a large saucepan or kettle with enough water to just cover. Simmer, covered, until very tender, about 20 to 30 minutes; then purée it, along with its cooking water, in several batches, in a blender or food processor.

Cut tomatoes into quarters or eighths. If fresh, place them in a saucepan and simmer until tender; if canned, use as is. Purée them.

Combine the two purées and transfer to a kettle. Add chicken stock and salt to taste. Simmer about 15 minutes.

To serve, ladle soup into individual soup bowls. Top each with a spoonful of Crème Fraîche or whipped cream. Sprinkle with minced arugula or watercress.

ARUGULA SOUP

Dark green and with a pleasantly sharp flavor, the current darling of our salad bowls, arugula has been gathered wild for centuries by Italian and French peasants (who call it rucola *and* roquette, *respectively). A friend recently told me that she thinks arugula is one of those things in life that's so good you feel there's never* quite *enough of it in any given serving.*

Like spinach or watercress, arugula is as good in the soup pot as the salad bowl.

Serves 6

2 bunches arugula (about 4
 cups [1000 ml] loosely
 packed leaves)
3 tablespoons (45 ml) butter
1 tablespoon (15 ml) flour

4 cups (1000 ml) chicken
 broth
2 cups (500 ml) milk
Salt

Rinse the arugula and shake dry. Cook it in a kettle with 2 tablespoons (30 ml) of the butter over low heat for 3 or 4 minutes, or until the arugula wilts and turns dull green. Transfer to a blender or food processor and purée it. Reserve.

Melt the remaining tablespoon (15 ml) butter in the kettle. Stir in flour and cook about a minute. Stir in chicken broth. Return arugula to the kettle and add milk. Add salt to taste. Simmer, uncovered, about 8 minutes.

ADVANCE PREPARATION: May be made several hours ahead of time and carefully reheated to serve.

CRAB CHOWDER WITH CRÈME FRAÎCHE AND LIME

Seafood chowders in one form or another are a dietary fixture wherever there is a seacoast. Of course, there are lots of debates along America's East Coast about whether "real" clam chowder should have a tomato or cream base. I don't much care myself, and I'm always happy to eat the best examples of either.

Serves 4

1 pound (450 g) fresh or frozen crabmeat
2 cups (500 ml) water
½ cup (125 ml) white wine
1 teaspoon (5 ml) minced fresh tarragon, or ¼ teaspoon (1.5 ml) dried

2 medium potatoes
1 small onion, finely minced
2 tablespoons (30 ml) butter
2 teaspoons (10 ml) fresh lime juice
4 cups (1000 ml) milk
Salt

GARNISH:

1 cup (250 ml) Crème Fraîche (see Cornmeal Crêpes with Crème Fraîche and Caviar for recipe)

Grated rind from 1 lime

Place ¼ cup (60 ml) of the crabmeat in a saucepan with 2 cups (500 ml) water, wine, and tarragon. Simmer, uncovered, for 10 minutes. Transfer mixture to a blender or food processor and purée it. Reserve.

Peel and dice the potatoes and cook them, along with the onions, in the butter in a kettle over medium-low heat until the onions begin to soften. Pour in the puréed crab mixture and simmer about 7 minutes, or until the potatoes are tender. Add lime juice, milk, and remaining crabmeat. Add salt to taste and simmer another 5 minutes.

To serve, blend Crème Fraîche and grated lime rind together. Ladle chowder into individual bowls and top each with a spoonful of Crème Fraîche mixture.

BEET BROTH WITH SOUR CREAM

Borshch, or borscht, or borsht is the national soup of Russia and Poland and, according to Leo Rosten in The Joys of Yiddish, *it was a great staple among Jews because beets were so cheap. "Billig vie borsht," or "cheap as borscht," the old saying goes. There are even more recipes for this beet-based soup than there are ways to spell it. The following adaptation is a simple and colorful way to begin a festive meal: try the ruby red broth as a first course for a Christmas dinner, followed by Duck with Black Pepper and Kumquats or Game Hens with Mole Sauce. Or serve it jellied, on a warm summer evening (see Variation).*

Serves 6

1 onion
1 medium clove garlic
5 to 6 medium beets, about 1 pound (450 g) total
5 cups (1250 ml) chicken broth

1 bay leaf
½ teaspoon (3 ml) dried dill
Salt

GARNISH:
1 cup (250 ml) sour cream
2 tablespoons (30 ml) grated horseradish, fresh or bottled (preserved in vinegar)

Chop onion, garlic, and beets coarsely. Place in a large saucepan or kettle with chicken broth. Add bay leaf and dill and simmer until beets are tender. Transfer soup to blender or food processor and purée it. Strain mixture back into the kettle, add salt, and reheat.

Stir sour cream and horseradish together. Ladle soup into individual bowls and top each with a spoonful of the sour cream mixture.

VARIATION: To serve the beet broth cold and jellied, dissolve 1 tablespoon (15 ml) gelatin in ⅓ cup (85 ml) warm water. Stir mixture into the soup just before puréeing. Chill strained broth until it is set. To serve, chop jellied soup into cubes, spoon into bowls, and top with sour cream mixture.

BUTTERNUT SOUP WITH ORANGE CRÈME FRAÎCHE

Fall means pumpkins, butternut and acorn squashes, and a host of other orange-fleshed gourds that symbolize All Saints' Day, Halloween, and the harvest festivals our rural ancestors celebrated. For a fine country or urban autumn dinner, serve this soup followed by Lasagne with Chicken and Marsala, Broccoli with Wasabi, and Honey-Quince Tart for dessert.

Serves 6 to 8

1 large butternut squash, about 1½ pounds (675 g)	1 bay leaf
1 medium onion, chopped	¼ teaspoon (3 ml) dried thyme
1 tablespoon (15 ml) sweet butter	¼ teaspoon (3 ml) dried sage
6 cups (1500 ml) chicken broth	Salt
	Pepper
	⅓ cup (85 ml) dry sherry

GARNISH:

½ cup (125 ml) Crème Fraîche (see Cornmeal Crêpes with Crème Fraîche and Caviar for recipe)	1 tablespoon (15 ml) grated orange rind

Cut squash in half and scrape out seeds. Peel and cut squash in cubes about 2 inches (50 mm) square.

In a kettle, cook onion in butter over medium heat until wilted. Add squash, chicken broth, and dry seasonings. Simmer, partly covered, until squash is very tender, about 30 minutes. Purée mixture, in batches, in a blender or food processor. Return to kettle, stir in sherry, and reheat.

To serve, stir together Créme Fraîche and grated orange rind. Ladle soup into individual serving bowls and top each with a spoonful of Créme Fraîche mixture.

CHILLED AVOCADO SOUP WITH BUTTERMILK

Buttermilk used to be a familiar ingredient in all rural households where butter was made. The milky liquid remaining after churning was the buttermilk. Today's buttermilk is something different, produced by fermenting skim milk with cultures similar to the ones used in yogurt. Buttermilk is low in fat, calories, and cholesterol and high in calcium. Its tangy, refreshing flavor makes an ideal base for cold soups. This is an ideal recipe to put together quickly after work, or to make on a summer day when the kitchen is too hot for cooking. On a day like that serve Tomatoes Niçoises and a big green salad following the soup, with champagne and peaches for dessert.

Serves 6

1 large ripe avocado
1 quart (1000 ml) buttermilk
1 teaspoon (5 ml) lemon or lime juice

⅛ teaspoon (.5 ml) cayenne pepper

OPTIONAL GARNISH:
2 tablespoons (30 ml) minced fresh cilantro or dill

1 lime, thinly sliced

Purée avocado, buttermilk, lemon juice, and cayenne in a blender or food processor. Refrigerate until ready to serve.

To serve, ladle soup into individual bowls and garnish with chopped herbs and lime slices if desired.

COLD CARROT SOUP WITH GUACAMOLE

Carrot soup, hot or cold, is always called Crécy *in France after the town by the same name in Seine-et-Marne, which is reputed to have excellent soil for growing carrots. The infamous Battle of Crécy, in which the flower of French youth was killed, was fought here in 1346; carrot soup is more or less a memorial to them. Add Guacamole to* potage Crécy *and you have a colorful, summery French-Mex soup.*

Serves 6

COLD CARROT SOUP:

1 onion, chopped
1 clove garlic, minced
1 tablespoon (15 ml) sweet butter
1 tablespoon (15 ml) oil
1 pound (450 g) carrots, sliced
1 teaspoon (5 ml) dried thyme
¼ teaspoon (1.5 ml) nutmeg
4 cups (1000 ml) chicken broth
½ cup (125 ml) whipping cream
Salt
Pepper

GUACAMOLE:

1 ripe avocado
2 tablespoons (30 ml) finely minced onion
2 teaspoons (10 ml) lemon juice
3 dashes Tabasco
Salt
Pepper

Cook onion and garlic in butter and oil in a kettle over low heat until onions are translucent. Add carrots and continue cooking another minute or two. Stir in thyme and nutmeg. Pour in chicken stock and simmer, partially covered, about 15 minutes, or until carrots are tender. Transfer mixture to blender or food processor, in batches if necessary, and purée it. Stir in cream. Add salt and pepper to taste. Chill mixture several hours or overnight.

To make Guacamole, mash avocado with a fork. Stir in remaining ingredients.

To serve, ladle soup into individual soup bowls. Top each with a spoonful of Guacamole.

SALADS

Let first the onion flourish there
Rose among roots, the maiden fair,
Wine scented and poetic soul
Of the capacious salad bowl.

Robert Louis Stevenson

The salad bowl, capacious or otherwise, has been accorded star status on contemporary menus. The full realization of this struck me a few years ago when I had lunch with a friend in the first California cuisine restaurant to open in New York. We each ordered salad: mâche and radicchio and slices of warm grilled lamb; endive with hot, smoky shiitake mushrooms and a sprinkling of pine nuts. They were dazzling salads, and we tried not to mind that they cost as much as a small sports car.

The elaborate salad with expensive ingredients was not invented in the late twentieth century, however. In *Kitchen and Table,* Colin Clair describes a salad served at a sixteenth-century Italian banquet that included among its ingredients ham, mullet roe, herring, tuna, anchovies, capers, olives, caviar, and candied flowers, the whole thing surmounted by turnips carved into castles.

Meanwhile, what were the peasants eating in the way of salads? During the growing season they ate greens and leafy plants of various kinds, often scavenged wild in fields and along streams. In ancient

Sumer and Egypt, watercress and other cresses, various lettuces, onions, garlic, and cucumber were part of the diet. In the Mediterranean world, olive oil has been used to dress salads since the beginning of agricultural history. By the time of medieval European civilization, salads had not changed all that much: a fourteenth-century English recipe for "salat" calls for such things as parsley, sage, garlic, onions, fennel, watercress, and mint to be mixed with olive oil. "Laye on vinegar and salt, and serve it forth," the recipe concluded. Throw in a few slices of warm lamb or duck, and you'll have a salad as chic as anything served in Paris or Manhattan today. *Plus ça change.* . . .

Papaya, Red Onion, and Apple Salad

Potato Salad with Radicchio

Leaf Lettuce with Cayenned Walnuts

Tomatoes with Balsamic Vinegar and Shallots

Mâche with Warm Shiitake Mushrooms

Green Bean Salad with Pesto

Tomatoes Niçoises

Cold Beets with Yogurt, Sour Cream, and Dill

PAPAYA, RED ONION, AND APPLE SALAD

The yellow-orange flesh of the papaya is as beautiful as it is delicious. This tropical fruit, discovered by Christopher Columbus in its native West Indies, contains an enzyme called papain, which is said to be beneficial to digestion and is used in granular form to tenderize meat. Filipino and other South Pacific and Asian cuisines have been using papayas in salads and pickles for hundreds of years.

This salad adds a refreshing and colorful note to any meal. Try it with Black Bean Cakes, or Game Hens or Quail with Mole Sauce.

Serves 4

½ ripe papaya
1 small red onion
1 medium green apple
5 tablespoons (75 ml) oil
3 tablespoons (45 ml) lemon
  juice

¼ teaspoon (3 ml) cumin
Salt
Pepper

OPTIONAL GARNISH:
  Romaine lettuce leaves

Peel papaya and remove seeds. Cut flesh in bite-sized pieces.
Peel the onion and slice it into very thin rounds.
Core and quarter the apple, but do not peel it. Slice it thinly.
Mix together oil, lemon juice, and cumin. Season to taste with salt
and pepper. Add papaya, onion, and apple and toss carefully. Let sit
about 10 minutes before serving, tossing it gently once or twice. Serve
as is, or on romaine leaves.

POTATO SALAD WITH RADICCHIO

*Sir Walter Raleigh is credited with bringing potatoes back from their
native South America and introducing them to Ireland. Unfortunately, only
starving Europeans and impoverished Colonists in the New World would
eat them—Europeans were convinced that potatoes were poisonous. Finally,
toward the beginning of the nineteenth century, Americans began to accept
potatoes as a routine part of their diet.*

*We've been slow to catch on to radicchio, too. This beautiful red-leafed,
white-ribbed member of the chicory family (which also includes Belgian
endive) has been enjoyed by Italian peasants and gentry alike for generations.
Its slightly bitter flavor and crunchy texture set off the potatoes nicely.*

Serves 6

About 2 pounds (900 g)
  small potatoes (red- or
  yellow-skinned variety)
6 green onions
1 small head radicchio
½ cup (125 ml) olive oil
3 tablespoons (45 ml) red or
  white wine vinegar

4 tablespoons (60 ml) dry
  white wine
1 teaspoon (5 ml) Dijon-
  type mustard
Salt
Pepper

OPTIONAL GARNISH:
1 cup (250 ml) cashew nuts,
   raw or roasted

Scrub potatoes. Boil or steam them until just tender when pierced with a small knife. Drain. As soon as they are cool enough to handle, slice them.

Trim roots and about 3 inches (75 mm) off the top of the green onions. Slice and combine in a bowl with the still-warm potatoes.

With a sharp knife, shred the radicchio. Add it to the potatoes.

In a small bowl, mix together oil, vinegar, wine, mustard, salt, and pepper. Pour over potatoes and toss gently. Taste for seasoning. (Some varieties of potato absorb much more liquid than others; if they seem too dry, add more oil and vinegar.)

Chop cashews coarsely and sprinkle over the top if desired.

ADVANCE PREPARATION: May be made several hours ahead of time. Or cook the potatoes the day before and mix them with the onions and dressing, adding the radicchio the next day.

LEAF LETTUCE WITH
CAYENNED WALNUTS

Bibb, Boston, red leaf, oak leaf, and butter lettuce are among the many different kinds of leaf lettuce (as opposed to head lettuce, such as iceberg) that are now available in American markets. Leaf lettuce is also the most popular type grown by American home gardeners. These are tender and mild compared to the wild greens gathered by peasant populations throughout history. But we too are probably softer and less assertive than were our ancestors.

Serve this salad before the meal, or following the main course the way Europeans do.

Serves 6

1 medium head leaf lettuce	Salt
6 tablespoons (90 ml) walnut oil or other mild-flavored oil	½ cup (125 ml) walnut halves
2 tablespoons (30 ml) wine vinegar	½ teaspoon (3 ml) cayenne pepper

Rinse lettuce leaves and dry carefully. Tear into bite-sized pieces and place in a bowl. Mix together 5 tablespoons (75 ml) of the oil, the vinegar, and salt.

Toss the walnuts with the remaining tablespoon (15 ml) of oil and the cayenne, adding a little more cayenne if you like things very spicy, less if you don't. Toast walnuts in broiler or toaster oven about 4 minutes, or until lightly browned.

Just before serving, toss the lettuce with the dressing. Arrange salad on six individual salad plates. Scatter a few walnuts over each.

TOMATOES WITH BALSAMIC VINEGAR AND SHALLOTS

This salad couldn't be simpler, but if good ripe tomatoes are available it echoes the epicurean perfection found in Provence or other warm-climate peasant cultures where platters of fresh tomatoes help measure out the summer days.

The tangy sweetness of balsamic vinegar complements the flavor of ripe tomatoes in this version of the classic recipe. Serve this with a meal when you don't want a green salad, or present it as a first course the way the French and Italians do. It is an excellent accompaniment to Crab with Wild Rice or Leg of Lamb with Pesto.

Serves 4

4 to 6 medium-sized ripe tomatoes

3 tablespoons (45 ml) olive oil

1 tablespoon (15 ml) balsamic vinegar

Salt

1 medium shallot, finely minced

Freshly ground black pepper

OPTIONAL GARNISH:
¼ cup (60 ml) minced parsley

Slice the tomatoes and arrange them in two or three overlapping rows on a serving platter. Combine olive oil, vinegar, and salt, and drizzle over the tomatoes. Scatter the minced shallots over the top and add a few grinds of pepper. Sprinkle with minced parsley if desired.

ADVANCE PREPARATION: May be made an hour or two in advance.

MÂCHE WITH WARM SHIITAKE MUSHROOMS

Field lettuce, lamb's lettuce, corn salad, and the French mâche are some of the names used to describe these tender, oval-leaved salad greens that French peasants have been harvesting for generations. Happily for us, American produce dealers are beginning to offer mâche, and many seed companies now carry the seed for home gardeners.

This is an excellent salad to serve as a first course at a dinner party. Follow it with Mussels in Saffron Sauce with Zucchini Timbales, or Linguine with Shrimp and Fresh Ginger.

Serves 4

1 large handful mâche, about 2 ounces (56 g)

6 to 8 fresh shiitake mushrooms, 3 to 4 ounces (84 to 112 g) total

3 to 4 tablespoons (45 to 60 ml) walnut or olive oil

1 tablespoon (15 ml) balsamic or red wine vinegar

1 small clove garlic, very finely minced

Salt

Pepper

⅓ cup (85 ml) pine nuts

Arrange mâche leaves in the bottom of a shallow bowl.

If mushrooms are very large, cut them in half. Brush them with about 1 tablespoon (15 ml) of the oil and broil them (or grill over coals) until they are very hot and limp.

Mix together the remaining oil, vinegar, garlic, salt, and pepper.

Toast the pine nuts in a toaster oven or in a heavy skillet (do not add oil) until lightly browned.

Just before serving, reheat the mushrooms if necessary and distribute them over the top of the mâche. Pour oil and vinegar mixture over them. Sprinkle pine nuts over the salad.

GREEN BEAN SALAD WITH PESTO

We Americans have a tendency to seize a good thing and then worry it to death like a puppy with a sock. Take the poor quiche, for example, a perfectly respectable peasant tart that came to us from Lorraine; by now every restaurant in the country has had a fling at it, piling on carrots and broccoli, clams and pineapple. At a party once I was even served quiche garnished with cocktail sausages and processed cheese, surely a new low in the history of quiches.

I'm afraid the same sort of thing may be happening to pesto, for I've already run into pesto-backlash here and there—people who say they're tired of pesto, they've stopped freezing it in ice-cube trays for winter use, they've ripped out their basil and planted rosemary instead. Oh, well. This is still an awfully good salad. Serve it at a buffet supper with Black Bean Cakes or Deep-dish Drumstick Pie. Or take it on a picnic.

Serves 6

2 pounds (900 g) green beans

2 cups (500 ml) fresh basil leaves

½ cup (125 ml) olive oil

3 tablespoons (45 ml) pine nuts

2 garlic cloves, minced

¼ cup (60 ml) grated Parmesan

3 tablespoons (45 ml) lemon juice

Salt

Trim and string the beans. Steam or simmer until tender but still crunchy, about 8 to 10 minutes. Drain and transfer beans to a large bowl.

Place remaining ingredients in blender or food processor and purée, stopping machine to scrape down sides of bowl if necessary. Pour mixture over beans and toss well.

Allow beans to sit several hours or overnight, tossing occasionally (beans may be left at room temperature for 2 to 3 hours, but should be refrigerated for longer periods). Serve cold or at room temperature.

ADVANCE PREPARATION: Make the salad the day before if possible to allow beans to absorb flavors.

TOMATOES NIÇOISES

Tomatoes, anchovies, and capers have been a standard combination in the regional cooking of Mediterranean France and Italy for hundreds of years. Pizzas and pissaladières *(a sort of Provençal pizza), salads, sandwiches, and pastas are all frequently flavored with this same mouth-watering combination. The following stuffed tomatoes make a wonderful lunch or first course for a summer dinner. Start with a cold soup such as Chilled Avocado Soup with Buttermilk or Cold Carrot Soup with Guacamole. Serve another salad with the tomatoes, such as Potato Salad with Radicchio.*

Serves 4 to 6

4 to 6 large ripe tomatoes	3 hard-boiled eggs
3 anchovies	1 tablespoon (15 ml) lemon
1 7-ounce (196-g) can	juice
white-meat tuna	1 tablespoon (15 ml) capers

GARNISH:
Mediterranean-style black olives

Cut a slice off the top of each tomato and scoop out the flesh with a spoon. Reserve the tomato flesh.

With a fork, mash the anchovies coarsely. Mash the tuna in with the anchovies. Stir in the tomato flesh. Chop the eggs and add them, along with the lemon juice and capers. Fill the emptied-out tomatoes with this mixture. Garnish with olives.

COLD BEETS WITH
YOGURT, SOUR CREAM, AND DILL

Beets and sour cream are a favorite combination in Balkan cuisine. This makes a colorful first course or even a side dish to serve with something with uncomplicated flavors, such as Lamb Tarts.

Serves 4

4 medium beets	2 teaspoons (10 ml) minced
½ cup (125 ml) sour cream	fresh dill, or ½ teaspoon
½ cup (125 ml) yogurt	(3 ml) dried
2 medium cloves garlic,	
finely minced	

Rinse beets and cut off stems. Simmer them in enough water to just cover, or wrap them in foil and bake at 400°F. until tender. Either process should take 30 minutes to 1½ hours, depending on size.

When beets are cool enough to handle, slip the skins off them. Trim a small slice off the bottom so they will have an even base to rest on. Cut a slice off the stem ends and, with a small, sharp knife, carefully hollow out the inside of the beets, leaving a shell 1½ inches (37 mm) thick (save the pieces to put in a salad).

Combine sour cream, yogurt, garlic, and dill and fill the hollowed-out beets with the mixture. Chill thoroughly.

SEAFOOD

. . . a piece of broiled fish, and of an honeycomb.

St. Luke 24:42

What do Bigmouth Buffalo, Yellowtail Jack, Wahoo, and Shortbelly have in common? No, it isn't a group of gangsters from the Far West —these are the names of different kinds of fish found in the Pacific. If you haven't heard of any of them, don't be surprised: there are so many different species of fish and shellfish in the world's waters that even if you ate a different kind for dinner every night for the rest of your life, you'd be unlikely to sample all the possibilities.

Until very recently Americans have tended to be unenthusiastic about seafood, but in virtually every other civilization people in all walks of life ate freshwater or saltwater fish as often as possible. Not only did streams, rivers, ponds, and oceans teem with fish, but aquaculture, or fish-farming, has been practiced since at least 2,500 years ago, when the Chinese were raising carp in specially maintained ponds.

For the world's peasants, seafood has literally been a lifesaver. In many societies where little other protein was available to the poor, it was often possible to net a fish somewhere, especially in the days before overfishing and pollution had depleted the waters' resources. In medieval Europe, fish could be found swimming in urban rivers—the Thames and the Seine even had breeding enclosures for various kinds of fish, especially trout and salmon. When techniques for salting and drying were perfected, fish became even more valuable as an inexpensive and virtually indestructible food that could be easily transported and stored for years (dried fish wasn't always easy to reconstitute, however; one old recipe recommends pounding dried fish with a hammer for an hour to tenderize it).

There are almost as many recipes for preparing seafood as there are, well, fish in the sea. The Chinese eat sweet-and-sour carp. Laotians make a catfish soup with chiles and eggplant. The Mexicans also like chiles with their fish—in a popular dish called Huachinango à la Veracruzana, red snapper is stewed with chiles and tomatoes. In Thailand seafood is often curried. The Japanese love raw seafood, or sashimi. In Southeast Asia it is not unusual to find fish cooked in banana leaves, and fish stews are seasoned with saffron in Spain and Provence.

Increased exposure to other cultures helped awaken the American taste for fish. Better refrigeration has improved our ability to transport and store seafood. Education about cooking methods has produced more palatable results. We now know that fish must be very fresh for good flavor, and that overcooking toughens fish and sometimes gives it an off-flavor. (Today's general rule of thumb is that fish should be cooked about 10 minutes for each inch (25 mm) of thickness; in other words, if your swordfish steak, say, is 2 inches (50 mm) thick, poach or broil it for 20 minutes.) With restaurants, magazines, and cookbooks introducing new varieties of seafood and exciting ways to prepare it, and especially with our passionate interest in health and slimness, we've become enthusiastic about seafood—the high-protein, low-fat, low-calorie food that is available in a variety of shapes and tastes and adapts deliciously to seemingly infinite methods of preparation.

Scallops with Braised Fennel

Fish Fillets with Macadamia Nuts and Guinness

Crab Cakes with Guacamole and
Cilantro-Lime Butter

Salmon with Soy Sauce and Lime

Scallop Terrine with Scallion Sauce

Curried Shrimp and Chicken with
Fresh Mint and Couscous

Cold Salmon Mousse with
Sour Cream–Romaine Dressing

Fish Mousse with Lobster and Saffron
Cream Sauce

Clams with Pesto

Crab with Wild Rice

Poached Cod with Fresh Sage Butter

Mussels in Saffron Sauce with Zucchini Timbales

Shad Roe with Sorrel Hollandaise

Fish Fillets Broiled with Mustard

Whole Wrapped Fish

Sea Scallops Wrapped in Spinach

See also:

Linguine with Shrimp and Fresh Ginger

SCALLOPS with BRAISED FENNEL

Fennel bulb—or, more properly, the enlarged leaf stalks at the base of the stem of the fennel plant—is a staple food in Provence and southern Italy (where it is called finocchio*). Its light anise flavor is traditionally paired with seafood.*

This is a light and delicate dish, so you could start the meal with something hearty—try Mâche with Warm Shiitake Mushrooms, or Eggplant–Garlic Soup. Serve the scallops with plain buttered rice and Tomatoes Stuffed with Goat Cheese.

Serves 4 to 6

2 medium fennel bulbs	4 tablespoons (60 ml) sweet
3 tablespoons (45 ml) olive oil	butter
3 medium cloves garlic, chopped	1 pound (450 g) bay scallops (or sea scallops cut in quarters)
About ½ cup (125 ml) water	½ cup (125 ml) white wine

Cut fennel in quarters. Place in a heavy skillet with olive oil and cook over medium heat, turning occasionally, until lightly browned. Add garlic and about ½ cup (125 ml) water to skillet. Cover and simmer about 45 minutes, turning fennel occasionally, until it is very tender and glazed. If liquid hasn't all been absorbed at end of cooking time, remove lid and continue cooking over higher heat, watching carefully to prevent burning. Remove fennel and reserve, but do not wash out skillet.

Just before serving, reheat fennel if necessary and remove to a serving platter. Add butter to skillet and heat until bubbly. Add scallops and cook, stirring constantly, about 3 to 4 minutes, or just until opaque clear through. Arrange scallops on platter with fennel, then deglaze skillet by adding wine and stirring over high heat for 2 to 3 minutes, scraping bottom and sides of pan. Pour sauce over scallops and fennel and serve immediately.

ADVANCE PREPARATION: Fennel may be cooked several hours ahead of time and carefully reheated at the last minute.

FISH FILLETS WITH
MACADAMIA NUTS AND GUINNESS

Our ancestors were eating nuts before they swung down from the trees to become peasants. Throughout history nuts have provided one of the most readily available sources of fat and calories for peasant populations—pine nuts in the Mediterranean, hickory nuts and pecans for Native Americans, pistachios in the Near East. Though widely cultivated in Hawaii, macadamia nuts are native to Australia. Add their rich flavor to that of dark beer, and ordinary fish fillets are lifted into the realm of the sublime.

Serve simple accompaniments with this—Carrot Tart with Spinach "Crust," for example, or Barley-Leek Gratin.

Serves 4

4 to 6 fillets of mild, white
fish (flounder, sole, scrod,
etc.), about 1½ to 2
pounds (675 to 900 g) total

⅓ cup (85 ml) Guinness stout
(or other rich, dark ale or
beer)

1¼ cups (310 ml) macadamia
nuts, coarsely chopped

1 tablespoon (15 ml) butter

Place fish in a single layer in a deep dish and pour stout over it. Let macerate 30 minutes to an hour. Arrange fish on a greased baking sheet. Sprinkle with chopped nuts and dot with butter. Place under the broiler for 5 to 8 minutes, depending on thickness of fish.

CRAB CAKES WITH GUACAMOLE AND CILANTRO-LIME BUTTER

The first European settlers in North America found so many crabs and lobsters along the eastern shore that they are said to have hauled off cartloads of them to plow into the fields as fertilizer! Every Colonial peasant kitchen along the Atlantic turned out crab cakes on a regular basis.

Serve Julienned Parsnips and Snow Peas with this, or Rice with Black-eyed Peas and Sun-dried Tomatoes.

Serves 4

CRAB CAKES:

1 pound (450 g) fresh or
frozen crabmeat

3 green onions, thinly sliced

½ red bell pepper, finely
minced

½ cup (125 ml) bread
crumbs or cracker crumbs

2 tablespoons (30 ml)
mayonnaise

1 tablespoon (15 ml)
Dijon-style mustard

1 egg, lightly beaten
Dash Worcestershire sauce
(optional)

GUACAMOLE:

1 ripe avocado

1 tablespoon (15 ml) lemon
juice

Dash Tabasco
Salt
Pepper

CILANTRO-LIME BUTTER:

½ cup (125 ml) butter   Salt
  Juice of ½ lime
2 tablespoons (30 ml)
  minced fresh cilantro

Mix together all ingredients for the crab cakes. Spoon mixture into four mounds on a generously oiled baking sheet, forming into patties with the back of a spoon. About 20 minutes before serving, place in a preheated 400°F. oven and bake until lightly browned, about 20 minutes.

To make Guacamole, with a fork, mash the avocado with lemon juice, Tabasco, salt, and pepper. Mixture should be a little lumpy.

To make Cilantro-Lime Butter, melt butter. Stir in lime juice, cilantro, and salt. Remove from heat immediately.

To serve, place a crab cake on each of four individual warmed plates. Top each with a spoonful of Guacamole. Spoon Cilantro-Lime Butter around each. Serve at once.

ADVANCE PREPARATION: Crab cakes may be formed a few hours in advance and kept refrigerated until baking. Guacamole may be made up to 2 hours in advance. To keep it from turning brown, store in the refrigerator in a covered bowl with the avocado seed on top of the Guacamole.

SALMON WITH SOY SAUCE AND LIME

Salmon was so abundant in the Atlantic at one time that Colonial farmers were known to feed their pigs an occasional salmon dinner. Those must have been very contented pigs.

You'll be happy too when you taste this dish, particularly if you can grill it. Serve it with rice or baked potatoes and Broccoli with Wasabi.

Serves 4

4 salmon steaks   2 tablespoons (30 ml) red
⅓ cup (85 ml) soy sauce   salmon roe (optional)
  Juice of 1 lime   1 lime, cut into wedges

Marinate salmon in soy sauce and the juice of one lime for at least 30 minutes (an hour or two is even better). Grill over very hot coals, or cook salmon in a very hot ungreased heavy skillet over medium-high heat, turning frequently. Remove to a serving platter, sprinkle roe over the top, and garnish with the lime wedges.

SCALLOP TERRINE WITH SCALLION SAUCE

Many French peasant dishes are baked in earthenware containers called terrines. They may be unmolded or served right from the baking dish.

Green onions are called different things in different places. Scallion and spring onion are common terms, but in parts of the South scallion means shallot. In Wales, scallion sometimes refers to a larger leek-like onion, otherwise known as the Welsh onion—which, incidentally, comes originally from Siberia. By any other name the scallions in this dish are green onions, and they should be added to the sauce only at the last minute; if overheated, they loose their vivid green color.

Serves 4 to 6

SCALLOP TERRINE:

1 bunch scallions (about 5 scallions)
1 pound (450 g) mild fish fillets (sole, flounder, cod, etc.)
⅓ cup (85 ml) fresh bread crumbs
⅓ cup (85 ml) milk
1 teaspoon (5 ml) sweet butter

2 whole eggs plus 1 egg white
¼ teaspoon (1.5 ml) nutmeg
½ teaspoon (3 ml) dried tarragon
Salt
½ pound (225 g) bay scallops (or sea scallops cut in quarters)

SCALLION SAUCE:

1 small shallot, minced
1 tablespoon (15 ml) sweet butter
⅔ cup (170 ml) white wine
⅓ cup (85 ml) water

2 tablespoons (30 ml) whipping cream
Reserved green tops from the scallions

Trim off roots and top inch or two (25 to 50 mm) from the scallions. Slice the white part only, reserving remaining green tops.

Cut fish fillets in 1-inch (25-mm) chunks. Place them along with the sliced scallion-whites in the food processor. Add all the remaining terrine ingredients except scallops. Purée until mixture is smooth.

Spread half the mixture in a terrine or loaf pan. Cover with the scallops. Spread the remaining mixture over them. Bake at 350°F. until mixture is set and beginning to color around the edges, about 45 to 50 minutes.

To make Scallion Sauce, cook shallot in butter until it is soft. Add wine, water, and cream and boil over medium-high heat for 5 minutes. Mince green scallion tops finely. Add to sauce and cook an additional 2 to 3 minutes. Serve immediately.

Serve terrine in slices, with a little sauce spooned around each.

CURRIED SHRIMP AND CHICKEN WITH FRESH MINT AND COUSCOUS

The curry powder we know in the West is certainly good, but it has almost nothing to do with the rich and varied blends of herbs and spices used in peasant and royal households alike in India. There, the combination of flavors ranges from utterly simple to concoctions so splendid that an Englishman writing in 1616 enthused that the curry he'd eaten made him "almost thinke it that very dish which Jacob made ready for his father, when he got the blessing."

Serve the usual curry accompaniments in individual serving bowls: chutney, unflavored yogurt, sliced scallions, chopped cucumber, peanuts, raisins, and so on.

This is a dish with both an Indian and a Middle Eastern accent. You could serve it with traditional plain or brown rice, but it is lighter and more interesting with couscous mixed in with the rice. Follow package directions for cooking the couscous grain (you can buy it in most grocery stores—it's usually next to the rice—or where Middle Eastern foods are sold).

Serves 6 to 8

2 tablespoons (30 ml) sweet butter	1 tablespoon (15 ml) flour
1 clove garlic, minced	2½ cups (625 ml) chicken stock
1 tablespoon (15 ml) commercial curry powder (or more, to taste), or make your own (see recipe below)	2 teaspoons (10 ml) finely minced fresh gingerroot
	⅛ teaspoon (.5 ml) cayenne pepper (or to taste)
	Salt

3 whole cooked boneless chicken breasts, skin and fat removed	2 cups (500 ml) cooked rice (⅔ cup [170 ml] uncooked)
1 pound (450 g) cooked, shelled shrimp	2 cups (500 ml) cooked couscous (1 cup [250 ml] uncooked)
2 tablespoons (30 ml) finely minced fresh mint	

CURRY POWDER

½ teaspoon (3 ml) dried coriander	½ teaspoon (3 ml) dried ginger
2 teaspoons (10 ml) cumin	½ teaspoon (3 ml) cardamom
1 teaspoon (5 ml) turmeric	¼ teaspoon (1.5 ml) cayenne
¼ teaspoon (1.5 ml) cinnamon	

Melt butter in a large skillet. Stir in garlic and curry powder and cook for about 1 minute, stirring, over low heat. Stir in flour and cook another minute. Whisk in chicken stock and simmer about 5 minutes. Add fresh ginger and cayenne. Taste for seasoning and salt to taste.

Cut chicken into bite-sized pieces and add to the skillet. About 8 minutes before serving, stir shrimp into the mixture. Simmer, stirring frequently, until shrimp is thoroughly cooked, about 5 to 8 minutes. Transfer to a warm serving bowl and sprinkle with fresh mint. Pass rice and couscous, mixed together, in a separate bowl.

ADVANCE PREPARATION: The curry sauce will be even better made a day in advance. You can even add the chicken to it and refrigerate overnight. But cook the shrimp just before serving.

COLD SALMON MOUSSE WITH SOUR CREAM-ROMAINE DRESSING

Fish loaves, put together from scraps of leftover fish mixed with bread or potatoes, have provided nourishment for people wherever there is fish. Seafood mousses, terrines, or pâtés are fancier versions of the same idea.

Garnished with green peppercorns and a fresh green sauce, this mousse makes an excellent luncheon or summer supper dish. Serve it with Potato Salad with Radicchio or Papaya, Red Onion, and Apple Salad.

Serves 6 to 8

SALMON MOUSSE:

1 envelope (1 tablespoon [15 ml]) gelatin

¼ cup (60 ml) cold water

½ cup (125 ml) boiling water

½ cup (125 ml) mayonnaise

1 tablespoon (15 ml) lemon juice

½ teaspoon (3 ml) paprika

3 green onions (white part only; reserve tops for dressing)

3 cups (750 ml) cooked salmon, bones and skin removed

⅔ cup (170 ml) whipping cream

½ cup (125 ml) sour cream

¼ (60 ml) cup green peppercorns (preserved in brine)

SOUR CREAM-ROMAINE DRESSING:

1 cup (250 ml) sour cream

1 tablespoon (15 ml) lemon juice

5 to 6 leaves romaine lettuce, minced

⅛ teaspoon (.5 ml) cayenne pepper

1 tablespoon (15 ml) sliced green onion tops

Place gelatin in a large bowl and stir in ¼ cup (60 ml) cold water. Add ½ cup (125 ml) boiling water and stir until gelatin is dissolved. Add mayonnaise, lemon juice, and paprika. Slice the green onions, adding the white part to the gelatin mixture and reserving 1 tablespoon (15 ml) of the green part for the dressing. Add the salmon and transfer mixture to a food processor.

Purée salmon mixture, whip cream until stiff and fold into salmon. Pour half of the mixture into an oiled loaf pan or mold. Pour the other half into a bowl. Refrigerate both mixtures until they begin to set, about 10 minutes.

Meanwhile, stir sour cream and peppercorns together. Spread this mixture in an even layer over the top of the salmon mousse in the loaf pan. Pour the remaining mousse over it, smoothing with a knife. Cover and refrigerate several hours or overnight.

To make the dressing, place all ingredients in a blender or food processor and process until smooth.

To serve, unmold the mousse on a serving platter. Serve in slices, passing the dressing in a separate bowl.

FISH MOUSSE WITH
LOBSTER AND SAFFRON-CREAM SAUCE

*Saffron (from the Arabic word for "yellow," za'fran) appears in any
number of peasant dishes around the world, from bouillabaisse to paella to
Indian curries and Persian lamb dishes. Extremely labor-intensive to produce (it is made from the minuscule stamens of crocus flowers), saffron is
the world's most expensive spice. But a little saffron goes a long way, and
a few threads of it have, over the centuries and through many cultures,
contributed pungent flavor and brilliant color to otherwise bland and color-
less foods.*

*One of the best ways to use up leftover fish is to tuck it into a mousse.
I once made this dish with leftover salmon and it was wonderful. The lobster
and saffron sauce can be made on its own, too, and served over rice. With
the mousse, it's a very rich dish, so serve something simple with it—
Black-eyed Peas with Garlic and Parsley would be good, or Julienned
Parsnips and Snow Peas.*

Serves 6

FISH MOUSSE:
- 2 cups (500 ml) cooked mild-flavored fish (salmon, sole, cod, etc.), bones and skin removed
- 3 eggs, separated
- 1 tablespoon (15 ml) lemon juice
- 2 tablespoons (30 ml) minced parsley
- ⅛ teaspoon (.5 ml) cayenne pepper

LOBSTER AND SAFFRON CREAM SAUCE:
- ½ to 1 teaspoon (3 to 5 ml) saffron (see Note)
- 1 cup (250 ml) white wine
- 2 cups (500 ml) whipping cream
- Salt
- 1 pound (450 g) lobster meat

NOTE: The strength of saffron varies considerably according to variety, age, and so on. Start with ½ teaspoon (3 ml) and taste the sauce
as you go along; if the saffron flavor is too mild, add more—but don't
overdo it. Many years ago a friend brought me a generous supply of
saffron from Spain. I, in my vast ignorance, figured that if a little was
good a lot would be better and proceeded to dump a couple of large

59

tablespoons of the stuff into a fish stew. The result was a bitter-tasting disaster.

To make the mousse, beat together the fish, egg yolks, lemon juice, parsley, and cayenne. Beat the egg whites until stiff peaks form and fold into the fish mixture. Pour into a well-buttered loaf pan and bake at 350°F. about 40 minutes.

To make the sauce, soak the saffron in the wine for about 5 minutes. Place the cream in a heavy skillet and bring to a boil. Pour in the wine and saffron and simmer, stirring frequently, about 15 minutes (add any juices that may have accumulated from the lobster). Taste for seasoning and salt to taste. Just before serving, stir in the lobster meat and simmer about 5 minutes.

Unmold the mousse onto a serving platter and pour the sauce around it. Serve immediately.

CLAMS WITH PESTO

Friends from Oregon came to visit us in Manhattan. As I threw the door open to greet them, they rushed past me saying, "Can't talk—have to get the clams in water!" They dashed into the kitchen, yanked a cooler from their suitcase and thrust the captive clams under running water. Only after ascertaining that the little bivalves were still thriving, if jet-lagged, could we exchange a proper greeting. From another compartment of this large suitcase they produced a container of freshly made pesto.

The clams they had brought were tender little Northwest Coast butter clams, but any clam suitable for steaming could be used for this aromatic variation on traditional steamed clams. That night we served a couple of bottles of California Chardonnay (from the bottom of our friends' suitcase, of course), a superb combination that made us all as happy as, well, clams.

Serve as a first course followed by something nautical such as Salmon with Soy Sauce and Lime, or get lots of clams, some wonderful bread, and a big green salad and make a meal of it.

Serves 4 to 6

4 **pounds (1800 g) clams**	1 **cup (250 ml) water**

PESTO SAUCE:

2 **cups (500 ml) fresh basil leaves**	2 **tablespoons (30 ml) pine nuts**
3 **medium cloves garlic, minced**	¾ **cup (180 ml) olive oil** **Salt**

To prepare the clams, scrub them well and steam in a large kettle with 1 cup (250 ml) of water until the clams open, about 6 to 10 minutes. Remove the clams but do not discard the cooking broth.

To make the pesto sauce, tear the basil into shreds and place it in a blender or food processor. Add garlic and pine nuts. With the machine running, pour in the olive oil in a steady stream. Add salt and process until thickened.

Boil the clam broth over high heat for 5 minutes. Add the pesto and simmer about 2 minutes.

Arrange the clams in a large serving bowl and pour the pesto sauce over them. Serve at once.

CRAB with WILD RICE

Along with corn, wild rice was one of the staple Native American grains. Although it is not really rice at all but a separate grain indigenous to North America, it is usually cooked and served like rice.

For a truly all-American dinner, start the meal with Corn Chowder with Tarragon. Pass a platter of Tomatoes with Balsamic Vinegar and Shallots with the crab dish and serve Cranberry-Apple Streusel for dessert. All the main ingredients in this meal are natives of the American continent.

Serves 4

CRAB:
½ cup (125 ml) minced onion
1 tablespoon (15 ml) sweet butter
1 tablespoon (15 ml) oil
1 cup (250 ml) white wine
1 tablespoon (15 ml) *each* minced fresh parsley, chives, and basil (or ½ teaspoon [3 ml] dried basil if fresh is unavailable)

1 pound (450 g) fresh or frozen crabmeat
1 cup (250 ml) pine nuts
Salt

WILD RICE:
1 cup (250 ml) raw wild rice
1 medium onion, minced
1 tablespoon (15 ml) sweet butter

1 tablespoon (15 ml) oil
4 cups (1000 ml) water
Salt

GARNISH:
1 bunch watercress

To make the crab, cook the onion in butter and oil until it is soft and translucent (do not let it brown). Pour in the wine and cook over high heat about 3 minutes, stirring occasionally. Stir in the herbs, crabmeat, pine nuts, and salt to taste, and simmer until just heated through. Do not overcook.

To make the wild rice, place the raw wild rice in a fine-meshed strainer and rinse under cold water. Cook the onion in butter and oil until it is soft. Pour in the wild rice and continue cooking for several minutes, stirring constantly. Pour in the water, add salt, cover the pot, and simmer for 40 minutes, or until rice is tender and all the liquid has been absorbed.

Rub the bottom and sides of a ring mold with oil. Pack the wild rice in it. Cover with foil and place in a baking pan. Pour 2 to 3 inches (50 to 75 mm) of water into the pan. Bake at 350°F. about 30 minutes, or until very hot clear through.

To serve, unmold the rice onto a serving platter. Pour the crab mixture into the center of the ring. Garnish the outside of the ring with watercress.

ADVANCE PREPARATION: You can assemble the wild rice mold a day or two before serving. Keep it covered, in the refrigerator, and put it in the oven about 40 minutes before serving.

POACHED COD WITH
FRESH SAGE BUTTER

Sage, an herb with a distinguished history, figured prominently not just in peasant stewing pots but in their medicine cabinets as well—the name, in fact, comes from the Latin salveo, *to heal. Sage was said to prevent tremors, improve vision, "strengthen sinews," and was even thought to be a sort of antidepressant: "Sage ... will prevent that sad depression of spirits," according to the old* Virtues of British Herbs. *Samuel Pepys agreed: "Sage mitigates grief," he wrote. This recipe for fish fillets topped with a buttery sage sauce is certainly capable of lifting spirits, but I don't know if that's due to the curative powers of sage or just because fresh sage tastes so good.*

Don't attempt to use dried sage, which, in generous amounts, tends to taste like hamster-cage shavings. If you can't find fresh sage in your own herb garden or at the market, try to get a little pot of it at the local nursery. Serve with Rice with Black-eyed Peas and Sun-dried Tomatoes or Barley-Leek Gratin.

Serves 4

4 cod fillets (or any other fairly mild-flavored fish), 1½ to 2 pounds (675 to 900 g) total
1 cup (250 ml) water
1 cup (250 ml) white wine
1 tablespoon (15 ml) lemon juice

1 bay leaf
6 tablespoons (90 ml) sweet butter
2 tablespoons (30 ml) minced fresh sage

Place fish in a skillet with water, wine, lemon juice, and bay leaf. Simmer, covered, 5 to 8 minutes, or until fish is just cooked through. With a slotted spoon, remove fish and keep warm.

Turn heat up to high under the skillet. Swirl in the butter and boil mixture over high heat about 10 minutes, or until reduced by about half. Add sage and cook another minute. Pour over fish and serve at once.

MUSSELS IN SAFFRON SAUCE WITH ZUCCHINI TIMBALES

Timbales and ramekins are individual baking dishes in which various preparations are baked and usually unmolded for serving. The foods prepared in them have also come to be called timbales. In peasant kitchens, where food seldom goes to waste, leftovers of this and that are minced, mixed with a little egg and maybe some cheese or bread crumbs, spooned into timbales, and baked. The following version of the genre looks as good as it tastes: a delicate green hill floating in a saffron pool flecked with orange mussels.

Buy the smallest mussels you can find. Serve as a first course at an elegant dinner party, or as the main course with rice or pasta on the side.

Serves 6

ZUCCHINI TIMBALES:
1 medium shallot, minced
1 tablespoon (15 ml) sweet butter

4 egg whites
1 medium clove garlic, minced

4 small zucchini, about 8 ounces (225 g) total, minced
1 egg yolk
¼ teaspoon (1.5 ml) nutmeg
Salt

Pepper
6 timbales, ramekins, or custard cups

MUSSELS:

1 quart (1000 ml) mussels, washed and scrubbed clean

½ cup (125 ml) white wine
¼ cup (60 ml) water

SAFFRON SAUCE:

1 medium shallot, minced
1 tablespoon (15 ml) sweet butter
1 teaspoon (5 ml) saffron threads

½ cup (125 ml) mussel cooking water
½ cup (125 ml) whipping cream

To make the timbales, cook shallot in butter over medium heat until shallot is soft. Add garlic and cook 1 minute. Stir in zucchini and continue cooking, stirring occasionally, about 8 minutes, or until zucchini is soft. Let mixture cool.

Meanwhile, beat egg whites until stiff peaks form. Transfer the cooled zucchini mixture to a food processor or blender. Add egg yolk, nutmeg, salt, and pepper, and purée mixture. Fold into egg whites.

Preheat oven to 375°F. Generously butter six individual timbales or other small baking dishes. Divide zucchini mixture among them and place in a baking pan containing 2 or 3 inches (50 to 75 mm) of boiling water. Bake at 375°F. for 20 to 25 minutes.

To cook the mussels, place them in a kettle with white wine and water. Cover and bring to a boil. Cook about 5 minutes, shaking pan occasionally, until the mussels open. Remove the mussels from the shells and reserve them, discarding shells. Discard any mussels that do not open. Boil cooking broth over high heat about 8 to 10 minutes, or until it has reduced to about ½ cup. Reserve.

To make sauce, cook the shallot in 1 tablespoon butter over medium-low heat until it is soft. Stir in the saffron. Add the mussel cooking broth and cream. Simmer about 5 minutes. Stir in the mussels and simmer just long enough to heat through.

To serve, unmold timbales in the center of each of six serving plates. Spoon sauce around each one.

ADVANCE PREPARATION: Timbale mixture and sauce may be made up to an hour in advance. Bake timbales and carefully reheat sauce just before serving.

SHAD ROE WITH
SORREL HOLLANDAISE

Shad and shad roe are symbols of spring in New England. You don't need much sorrel for this recipe—a few leaves will do. Serve the traditional accompaniments, plain asparagus and boiled new potatoes, but give the traditionalists a delicious shock with Poached Meringues in Strawberry Sauce instead of the usual strawberries in cream or strawberry shortcake.

Serves 4

2 **medium pairs shad roe**
4 **tablespoons (60 ml) butter**

1½ **to 2 cups (375 to 500 ml)**
   fresh sorrel leaves

SORREL HOLLANDAISE:
2 **egg yolks**
½ **cup (125 ml) butter**
   Salt

1 **tablespoon (15 ml) lemon**
   juice
   Dash cayenne pepper

In a heavy skillet, cook the roe in 4 tablespoons (60 ml) butter about 5 minutes on each side, turning them once or twice. Regulate heat as necessary, and cover pan if the splattering is extreme.

Meanwhile, rinse the sorrel leaves and place them in a kettle over low heat; do not add more water to the leaves. Cover pot and cook about 2 minutes, or until leaves have just wilted. Transfer to a blender or food processor and purée.

Place egg yolks in a blender or food processor. Melt ½ cup (125 ml) butter until it is bubbly, then pour it slowly into the blender while machine is running. Season with salt, lemon juice, and cayenne. Fold puréed sorrel into mixture.

ADVANCE PREPARATION: Hollandaise sauce may be made up to 2 hours ahead of time and kept warm in a small wide-mouthed thermos. Do not attempt to reheat it or it will separate.

FISH FILLETS
BROILED with MUSTARD

Whether you've been working in the fields all day or trading on Wall Street, a quick and simple dinner is what you'll want to prepare when you get home. These fillets are the perfect answer. Put some rice on to cook, or toss some potatoes into the microwave to bake. Assemble Broiled Mushrooms Stuffed with Goat Cheese to stick under the broiler or in the oven while the fish cooks, and serve champagne with peaches for dessert.

Serves 4 to 6

6 to 8 fillets of white fish (such as sole, flounder, cod, etc.), about 2 to 3 pounds (900 to 1350 g) total

1 teaspoon (5 ml) Dijon-type mustard

1 tablespoon (15 ml) lemon juice

Dash cayenne pepper

Lemon wedges

Arrange fish in a single layer on an oiled baking sheet. Stir mustard, lemon juice, and cayenne together and brush mixture over fish.

Place fish in a preheated broiler and cook 3 to 5 minutes, depending on thickness of fish, or until it is opaque clear through. Garnish with lemon wedges.

WHOLE WRAPPED FISH

A whole fish, wrapped in banana leaves and grilled, is a traditional dish all over the Pacific basin. Banana leaves aren't easy to come by in most other regions, but aluminum foil, that splendid achievement of twentieth-century technology, offers an efficient alternative, sealing in flavors and juices during cooking to yield a juicy, aromatic fish. Use a mixture of fresh herbs if possible, otherwise parsley alone will do. Serve Potato-Mushroom Gratin with this, along with Sesame Spinach and Tomatoes with Balsamic Vinegar and Shallots.

Serves 1

1 small, cleaned, whole fish (such as trout, whiting, snapper, porgy, fresh mackerel, etc.), about ½ pound (225 g)

1 tablespoon (15 ml) minced fresh herbs (parsley, dill, chives, tarragon)

1 teaspoon (5 ml) sweet butter

1 teaspoon (5 ml) lemon juice

Aluminum foil

Lemon slices

Cut aluminum foil into a square big enough to wrap fish in. Place fish in the center of the piece of foil. Distribute herbs, 1 teaspoon (5 ml) butter cut in tiny pieces, and lemon juice both inside the fish and over its top surface. Gather up the sides of the foil and seal, leaving about an inch (25 mm) of air space between foil and the top of the fish.

Grill packet over charcoal or bake in a preheated 350°F. oven about 20 to 30 minutes, depending on size of fish. Allow about 10 minutes for each inch (25 mm) of thickness of fish, plus another 5 minutes for heat to penetrate foil; in other words, a fish about 2 inches (50 mm) thick will require about 25 minutes' cooking time.

To serve, slit open the top of packet with scissors or a sharp knife, and serve fish in its open packet.

ADVANCE PREPARATION: Fish may be wrapped several hours before cooking and refrigerated.

SEA SCALLOPS WRAPPED IN SPINACH

Even the humblest Japanese peasant is familiar with foods wrapped in attractive edible packaging. A thin sheet of seaweed is commonly used for this purpose, but bright green spinach leaves also make a handsome casing. Select spinach with the largest leaves possible for this. Serve as a first course, or with plain rice or Brown Rice Pilau as an entrée.

Serves 2 to 4

2 bunches spinach, about 1½ pounds (675 g) total

½ pound (225 g) sea scallops

Juice of 1 lemon

2 tomatoes, peeled, seeded, and chopped

GARNISH:
Lemon wedges
Soy sauce

Remove largest outer spinach leaves, reserving smaller inner leaves for another use. Wash the leaves and place them in a large kettle. Cover and steam over low heat about a minute, or until they are just beginning to soften. Do not let them get too limp. Lay each leaf out carefully on a work surface, overlapping two or three leaves if necessary. Place a scallop in the center of each leaf, squeeze a few drops of lemon juice over it, and top with a few pieces of tomato. Fold spinach carefully over each scallop to enclose it. Arrange the packets in a single layer in the bottom of a buttered baking dish. Cover and bake at 350°F. for about 8 minutes. Garnish with lemon wedges and pass soy sauce separately.

POULTRY

From the low peasant to the lord,
Turkey smokes on every board.

John Gay

Indigenous to North America, turkeys were very much a staple in Native American diets by the time the Europeans arrived. New England and Plains tribes caught the birds wild; in the West, Southwest, and Mexico they were domesticated early on. Turkey became popular in Europe very quickly but never supplanted the chicken as number-one favorite fowl.

Domestic chicken evolved in India, which may be where ducks were first domesticated, too. Or maybe it was in China—at any rate, Chinese peasants were among the first to raise ducks in captivity. Duck has always been popular in China, where there are probably more recipes for preparing it than anywhere else in the world. Curiously, the Japanese are not crazy about duck. The most highly regarded bird in Japan is quail, once reserved for royalty but now raised commercially and therefore within reach of almost everyone, at least occasionally. But chicken remains the most commonplace fowl in Japan, like everywhere else.

Goose is a more traditional food in Eastern Europe and parts of France than in the West. A few epicures believe that the only worthwhile part of the goose is its liver, used to make pâté and foie gras (literally "fat liver"). The taste for fat-logged goose liver has led to some unpleasant practices, at least from the goose's point of view: in France the animal's feet were nailed to the floor so that it could be force-fed, while in Russia geese were hung up in bags for a few days to prevent them from working off any of their fat.

Peasants had the unsavory task of forcing mash down the goose's gullet, but seldom did they eat the resulting fatted liver themselves: foie gras has always been an expensive delicacy. Feeding chickens was a simpler matter since they were often just left to forage on their own. But in some cultures chickens are fed special grains that are believed to improve the taste of the flesh. The Vietnamese like to give their chickens raw rice, which they say produces a juicier breast, while in southwestern France the birds eat corn, resulting in fine yellow flesh (poultry producers in the United States try to achieve this effect by feeding the chickens marigold petals). In Russia chickens raised on walnuts were thought to be especially succulent.

No matter what it's been eating, one of the main culinary attributes of chicken is its bland taste, which enables it to absorb other flavors easily and thereby be assimilated into just about everyone's national diet. In Oriental countries chicken is boned, chopped into small pieces, and stir-fried with any number of other seasonings and ingredients. In India chicken is commonly curried or cooked in a tandoor oven, but there are many other fine Indian ways of preparing it that are less familiar to Westerners—marinated and cooked with fresh coriander and ginger, for example. One of the best-known French peasant recipes, coq au vin, features chicken stewed with mushrooms and wine; it might be cooked with apples and cream in Normandy, with sauer-kraut in Alsace, and with tomatoes and olives in Nice. Chicken is the most popular meat in Indonesia, where it is often stewed with coconut. In West Africa, where chicken is traditionally served to an honored guest, it might be covered with peanut sauce, or stewed with okra, or roasted whole with yam stuffing.

Poultry is ideal for today's diet. White-meat chicken and turkey, especially with all skin and fat removed, are lower in fat, calories, and cholesterol than are red meats. Poultry adapts to any number of different preparations and can even substitute for veal or pork in many traditional recipes. Boneless chicken breasts are readily available, easy to prepare, and very quick-cooking.

Had Henry IV's wish that "there would not be a peasant so poor in all my realm who would not have a chicken in his pot every

Sunday" come true, France would have been a nation of universally well-off, well-fed, and healthy citizens.

Chicken Breasts with Braised Shallots, Prosciutto, and Raspberry Vinegar

Chicken with Fresh Figs, Port, and Basil

Duck with Black Pepper and Kumquats

Duck with Fettuccine, Cracklings, and Fresh Coriander

Game Hens or Quail with Mole Sauce

Deep-dish Drumstick Pie

Roast Chicken with Garlic and Fresh Ginger

Chicken Breasts with Lime and Orange Juice

Chicken with Watercress-Cream Sauce

Chicken Shepherd's Pie

Cold Chicken en Gelée

Rabbit in White Wine with Fresh Sage

Duck with Pears

See also:

Lasagne with Chicken and Marsala

Chicken Liver Soufflé with Fresh Tomato Sauce

CHICKEN BREASTS with BRASED SHALLOTS, PROSCIUTTO, and RASPBERRY VINEGAR

Shallots have been with us a long time. According to Theodora FitzGibbon's Food of the Western World, *this lavender-blushed member of the onion family came originally from Palestine and was mentioned in the Old Testament. Crusaders brought shallots back to Britain in the thirteenth century. One further note from Ms. FitzGibbon of potential interest to gardeners: shallots are traditionally planted on the shortest day of the year and lifted from the ground on the longest. With that in mind, perhaps this dish should be called "Chicken à la Equinox."*

Serves 4

4 boneless chicken breasts, about 3 pounds (1350 g) total
Wooden toothpicks
¼ pound (112 g) thinly sliced prosciutto
8 to 10 medium shallots, about 8 ounces (225 g)
1 tablespoon (15 ml) oil
1 tablespoon (15 ml) sweet butter
½ pound (225 g) mushrooms, sliced
¼ cup (60 ml) raspberry vinegar
½ cup (125 ml) chicken stock
Salt

Remove all skin and fat from the chicken breasts. Pound them with the edge of a plate or sturdy tumbler to flatten them. Lay a slice of prosciutto on top of each piece of chicken and roll it up into a cylinder. Hold it closed with toothpicks.

Peel the shallots, leaving them whole. Cook them in the oil and butter in a heavy skillet over medium heat for 4 to 5 minutes, turning frequently. Add mushrooms and continue cooking another 2 to 3 minutes, or until they and the shallots begin to brown. Raise heat if necessary to evaporate any accumulated juices.

With the heat on medium-high, pour in the raspberry vinegar, stirring to scrape up browned bits from bottom and sides of skillet. Add the chicken breasts and continue cooking a few minutes, turning frequently, until chicken begins to brown. Pour in the chicken stock and add salt to taste. Lower heat, cover the pan, and simmer 20 to 30 minutes, until chicken is very tender and juices have reduced to a syrupy consistency (remove cover and raise heat if necessary).

CHICKEN with FRESH FIGS, PORT, and BASIL

As far as I'm concerned fresh figs, which are indigenous to Arabia, still conjure up the exotic beauty and fantasy of the Arabian Nights with their pale green or port-wine flesh and scattering of golden seeds. They're a luxury today, but in ancient Egypt and classical Greece and Rome, all the way through medieval Europe, figs, fresh and dried, provided one of the most readily available sources of sugar for peasants and royalty alike.

Serve this dish with wild rice or plain rice, or with Barley-Leek Gratin.

Serves 4

2 boneless chicken breasts, about 1½ pounds (675 g) total

2 tablespoons (30 ml) sweet butter

½ cup (125 ml) white wine

½ cup (125 ml) port

2 tablespoons (30 ml) minced fresh basil, or ½ teaspoon (3 ml) dried

4 fresh figs, white or black, cut in quarters

Cut chicken breasts in half and remove all skin and fat. Cover each piece with waxed paper or plastic wrap and pound them with a kitchen mallet or other heavy object (such as a sturdy tumbler) until they are about ½ inch (12 mm) thick.

Melt butter in a heavy skillet. Add chicken and cook over medium heat for about 2 minutes, or until chicken turns white on the bottom. Turn and cook on the other side another couple of minutes. Add white wine, then cover skillet and simmer 10 to 15 minutes, or until chicken is cooked clear through. Remove chicken to a platter and reserve.

Raise heat under skillet and boil contents, stirring frequently, until reduced by about half. Add port and basil and continue cooking over medium-high heat for about 4 minutes, or until liquid has slightly reduced. Return chicken breasts to pan, reheat thoroughly, then arrange them on a serving platter. Garnish with quartered figs and pour sauce over all.

ADVANCE PREPARATION: Chicken may be cooked an hour or two in advance, then reheated and garnished with figs at the last minute.

DUCK WITH
BLACK PEPPER AND KUMQUATS

In the days before refrigeration—that is to say, throughout most of history—food was frequently rancid, if not downright spoiled, requiring huge quantities of spices to make it palatable. Pepper, which was the most sought-after of all spices, became so valuable that it was used as negotiable currency in the Middle Ages. Today, of course, pepper is one of the few bargains around, and an amount that might have bought you a tame elephant a few hundred years ago can be rubbed into the birds in this recipe with complete abandon. Although you may feel like Alice in Wonderland's Duchess as you rub a can of pepper into the ducks, the end result is worth the sneezing: pepper draws out the fat, leaving a crisp and spicy skin that is not overwhelmingly peppery.

This recipe makes an unusually attractive Christmas dish. For a festive holiday meal you might want to start out with Beet Broth with Sour Cream and Horseradish, then serve Lima Bean Purée with Rosemary and Buttermilk, and Carrots with Honey and Fresh Mint along with the ducks. Finish the meal with a flaming Cranberry Christmas Pudding.

Serves 4 to 6

2 ducks, 4½ to 5 pounds (2025 to 2250 g) each
1 2-ounce (56 g) can ground black pepper

2 medium-sized tart green-skinned apples, such as Granny Smith
2 medium onions

ORANGE-DUCK SAUCE:
Giblets and necks from ducks
1 small onion
1½ cups (375 ml) water
1 bay leaf
½ teaspoon (3 ml) thyme

1 cup (250 ml) white wine
⅓ cup (85 ml) Grand Marnier or other orange liqueur
Salt

KUMQUATS:
About ½ pound (225 g) fresh kumquats

½ cup (125 ml) sugar
1 cup (250 ml) water

Remove neck and giblets from cavity of ducks and reserve. Rinse ducks and pat dry. Prick them all over with a fork so the fat can drain out during cooking. Rub the ducks generously with the pepper, using about half the can per duck.

Preheat oven to 350°F. Core the apples but do not peel them. Cut apples and onions into quarters. Place half the onions and apples inside each duck. Arrange ducks on a rack in a roasting pan, breast side up. Bake in a 350°F. oven about 30 minutes per pound (450 g), or until the skin is nicely browned and crisp.

To make the sauce, place the giblets and necks in a saucepan with 1 whole onion and 1½ cups (375 ml) water. Add bay leaf and thyme and simmer, covered, for 30 minutes. Strain mixture into a clean saucepan. Add wine and boil over high heat about 5 minutes.

To prepare the kumquats, place them, whole, in a saucepan with the sugar and 1 cup (250 ml) water. Bring to a boil and simmer, uncovered, for 5 minutes. Turn off heat, cover the pan, and let sit for 10 minutes. Remove kumquats with a slotted spoon and reserve until needed.

When the ducks have finished cooking, remove them to a cutting board and keep warm. Pour off all the grease from the roasting pan. Pour the giblet-cooking sauce into the roasting pan, add the Grand Marnier, salt to taste, and cook over medium-high heat for 3 to 4 minutes, scraping up the brown bits from the bottom of the roasting pan. Pour into a sauceboat.

To serve, carve the ducks and arrange pieces on a warmed serv0 ing platter. Surround them with the kumquats. Pass the sauce separately.

DUCK WITH FETTUCCINE, CRACKLINGS, AND FRESH CORIANDER

Fresh coriander, or cilantro, may appear to be just an obscure herb gone suddenly trendy, but in fact it has added spice to Mexican, Indian, Vietnamese, and Caribbean foods for ages. It has a very distinctive flavor that some people, I'm told, find offensive; for the rest of us it's irresistible.

Serve a soup as a first course—Eggplant-Garlic, for example—and Papaya, Red Onion, and Apple Salad with the duck.

Serves 6

1 duck, about 4½ to 5 pounds (2025 to 2250 g)	2 cups (500 ml) chicken stock

½ cup (125 ml) white wine
1 onion, cut in half
1 large clove garlic, peeled
1 teaspoon (5 ml) minced
 fresh sage, or ½ teaspoon
 (3 ml) dried
 Salt

1½ pounds (675 g) spinach
 fettuccine
½ cup (125 ml) heavy
 cream
⅓ cup (85 ml) minced
 cilantro

OPTIONAL GARNISH:
 About 12 slices fresh
 pineapple

2 tablespoons (30 ml) butter

Cut the duck in quarters, or have the butcher do it. Using your fingers and sharp scissors, pull and cut off as much skin as possible. Discard all the fat you can pull off the duck, but save the pieces of skin to make cracklings.

Place the duck in a large kettle with chicken stock, white wine, onion, garlic, sage, and salt. Simmer, covered, about an hour, or until duck is cooked through and tender. Remove duck and strain broth into a clean saucepan. Boil over medium-low heat, uncovered, for about 30 minutes, or until it has reduced by about a third. Skim as much fat as possible from the surface.

When the duck is cool enough to handle, remove meat from bones, discarding any remaining fat and skin. Cut meat in 1-inch (25-mm) pieces and reserve.

Meanwhile, place the pieces of duck skin in a heavy skillet and cook over medium heat until crisp and golden (this can take up to 40 minutes; turn once or twice and cover skillet if it spatters severely). Drain cracklings on a paper towel, cut into bite-sized pieces, and reserve.

Just before serving, put the fettuccine on to cook. Add the pieces of duck and the cream to the duck broth. Bring to a boil while the fettuccine is cooking. Reheat the cracklings if necessary in a skillet, under the broiler, or in a toaster oven.

When pasta is cooked, drain it and return it to the kettle. Add the duck mixture and toss well. Pour onto a serving platter and sprinkle with cilantro and cracklings.

Optional garnish: Cook the pineapple in butter in a heavy skillet over high heat, turning occasionally, until pineapple is lightly browned. Pour any juices remaining in the pan over the duck mixture. Garnish the platter with the pineapple slices.

GAME HENS OR QUAIL WITH
MOLE SAUCE

In the days when most European woods and forests were owned by the aristocracy, game was available only infrequently to the peasant—"poached" wildfowl in those days didn't refer to the cooking method. Today, of course, most woodland has been given over to suburban development, and most of us buy our game from the butcher. Domestic quail is sometimes available; American-hybridized Rock Cornish game hens always are.

Turkey served with a rich, dark, chocolate-spiked sauce, mole de guajolote, *is a favorite Mexican dish. "It would be impossible to say just how many versions there are," writes Diana Kennedy in* Cuisines of Mexico. *"Every cook from the smallest hamlet to the grandest city home has her own special touch . . ." Some versions call for more of this or less of that, others like it hotter, or milder. The arguments go on forever according to Ms. Kennedy. But few would argue that the basic combination of chocolate, chilies, nuts and spices is unbeatable.*

Serves 4

4 game hens or quail

MARINADE:

1 medium clove garlic
1 tablespoon (15 ml) soy
sauce

1 teaspoon (5 ml) dried
thyme

STUFFING:

2 tablespoons (30 ml) raisins
¼ cup (60 ml) port
1 small onion, finely minced
½ red bell pepper, minced
1 tablespoon (15 ml) oil
2 medium cloves garlic,
minced
Livers from the game hens
or quail

2 ounces (56 g) pine nuts
(about ½ cup [125 ml])
2 cups (500 ml) cooked
brown rice (about ⅔ cup
[170 ml] uncooked)
½ teaspoon (3 ml) dried
thyme

77

MOLE SAUCE:

⅓ cup (85 ml) pumpkin seeds or unskinned almonds (about 2 ounces [56 g])

1 tablespoon (15 ml) sesame seeds, or 1 tablespoon (15 ml) tahini (see Note)

1 medium clove garlic, minced

1 corn tortilla, torn in shreds

2 small hot dried red peppers, or 1 pasilla pepper

⅛ teaspoon (.5 ml) cloves

½ teaspoon (3 ml) cinnamon

1 tablespoon (15 ml) chili powder

2 squares (2 ounces [56 g]) bitter chocolate

2 cups (500 ml) chicken stock

NOTE: Tahini, or sesame-seed paste, is found in stores that carry Middle-Eastern foods. Health-food stores also carry it.

Clean game hens or quail, removing livers and gizzards; reserve livers for later use.

Combine all ingredients for marinade.

Place game hens or quail in a deep dish with the marinade, rubbing the birds all over with the mixture. Let sit about 30 minutes.

Meanwhile, prepare the stuffing: Soak the raisins in the port for at least 10 minutes. Cook onion and bell pepper in oil about 3 minutes, then add garlic and reserved livers. Continue cooking another 3 to 4 minutes over medium heat, stirring and mashing the livers. Add the pine nuts and cook another 2 or 3 minutes. Transfer mixture to a bowl with the brown rice and stir in thyme and the raisins with the port. Stuff the birds with this mixture.

Preheat oven to 375°F. Place the birds on a rack in a roasting pan. Roast game hens about 40 minutes, quail about 30.

While they cook, make the sauce. Place pumpkin seeds, sesame seeds or tahini, garlic, tortilla, hot peppers, cloves, cinnamon, and chili powder in food processor or blender. Heat chocolate and chicken stock in a saucepan, over low heat, until chocolate melts. With processor running, pour in chocolate mixture. Return sauce to saucepan and simmer, uncovered, about 10 minutes.

To serve, arrange birds on a serving platter and spoon a band of sauce over each one. Pass remaining sauce separately.

DEEP-DISH DRUMSTICK PIE

Poultry pies are an ever-popular dish in many peasant cultures. Think of our own chicken potpies, or the Moroccan pigeon pie, b'stilla, for example. This dark and rich turkey drumstick pie conjures up the game pies still popular in the British countryside.

This is an excellent party dish. Serve it with a tossed green salad and Tomatoes Baked with Goat Cheese.

Serves 8 to 10

4 **turkey drumsticks, 4½ to 5 pounds (2025 to 2250 g) total**

2 **tablespoons (30 ml) oil**

2 **tablespoons (30 ml) butter**

2 **large onions, quartered**

2 **pounds (900 g) carrots, sliced**

3 **large cloves garlic**

2 **teaspoons (10 ml) fresh thyme, or 1 teaspoon (5 ml) dried**

2 **cups (500 ml) water**

2 **ounces (56 g) dried boletus (porcini) mushrooms**

1 **cup (250 ml) water**

1 **tablespoon (15 ml) flour**

1 **bay leaf**

1 **cup (250 ml) red wine**

1 **bunch leeks (about 3 leeks)**

½ **pound (225 g) thinly sliced prosciutto**

PIE CRUST:

2 **cups (500 ml) unbleached flour**

¼ **pound (112 g) butter, cut in 8 pieces**

1 **teaspoon (5 ml) salt**

In a large casserole, lightly brown the drumsticks on all sides in 1 tablespoon (15 ml) each of the butter and oil. Add the onions, half the carrots, and 3 whole cloves garlic. Continue cooking over medium-low heat another few minutes, until vegetables begin to color. Stir in the thyme, add 2 cups (500 ml) water, and simmer, covered, about an hour, or until turkey is tender. Remove turkey to a plate, reserving its cooking liquid.

Meanwhile, soak the mushrooms in 1 cup (250 ml) hot water for at least 30 minutes.

When turkey is cool enough to handle, remove the meat from the bones, cutting it in bite-sized pieces and discarding all fat, skin, and bones.

Place the turkey cooking liquid along with its vegetables in a food processor or blender (in batches if necessary) and process until smooth.

Place remaining 1 tablespoon (15 ml) each of butter and oil in the kettle. When heated, add the flour and stir over low heat about 1 minute. Stir in the turkey cooking liquid, the mushrooms and their soaking liquid, bay leaf, and red wine. Cook over medium heat about 20 minutes, or until liquid has reduced by about one-third and has thickened slightly.

Rinse the leeks carefully to get rid of all grit, and slice them. Add them along with remaining carrots to the sauce and simmer, uncovered, about 10 minutes, stirring occasionally. Stir in the cut-up turkey pieces. Mince the prosciutto and add it. Simmer about 5 minutes. Transfer mixture to a large baking dish.

To make the pie crust, mix together the flour, butter, and salt until mixture resembles coarse meal. Add just enough water for mixture to hold together. (This may all be done in the food processor, but be sure not to overmix or the crust will be tough.) Roll out dough about ½ inch (12 mm) larger than the edges of the baking dish. Lay it over the top of the dish, roll edges in and crimp them with a fork. Prick in a few places with a fork.

Bake in a preheated 350°F. oven about 45 to 50 minutes, or until crust has browned and filling is hot and bubbly.

ADVANCE PREPARATION: The entire dish may be made ahead of time and refrigerated for 2 or 3 days or frozen for up to 4 weeks.

ROAST CHICKEN WITH
GARLIC AND FRESH GINGER

The marriage of chicken and garlic is a felicitous one. Chicken cooked with 40 cloves of garlic (or 20, or 60—it doesn't matter, really) is an old favorite in French regional cuisine. Many people believe garlic has medicinal properties—if so, this dish is as good for the body as it is for the soul. Serve a green vegetable with this, such as Broccoli with Wasabi, and pass a platter of Tomatoes with Balsamic Vinegar and Shallots.

Serves 4

1 whole chicken, about 2½
  pounds (1125 g)
5 medium cloves garlic,
  minced

⅓ cup (85 ml) soy sauce
⅓ cup (85 ml) lemon juice
1 tablespoon (15 ml) grated
  gingerroot

Rinse chicken and pat dry. Combine remaining ingredients and rub about half of it over chicken, inside and out. Place chicken on a rack in a roasting pan and cover loosely with foil. Bake at 350°F. about 15 minutes, then baste with rest of soy sauce mixture. Continue roasting, uncovered, basting once or twice with pan drippings, about 30 to 40 minutes, or until drumstick feels loose when jiggled and juices run clear when chicken is pricked with a fork.

CHICKEN BREASTS WITH LIME AND ORANGE JUICE

Limes are used regularly to bring out flavor in Mexican and Pacific Basin foods. This simple dish is refreshing and very low in fat and calories. Serve it with Brown Rice Pilau, and Mâche with Warm Shiitake Mushrooms to start with.

Serves 4 to 6

2 whole boneless chicken
  breasts, 2 to 3 pounds (900
  to 1350 g) total
1 cup (250 ml) fresh orange
  juice

⅓ cup (85 ml) fresh lime
  juice
Rind of 1 lime
½ cup (125 ml) white wine

Remove all skin and fat from chicken breasts and cut them in half. With a sharp knife, cut three or four diagonal slashes across the surface of each piece of chicken and arrange them in a baking dish. Pour combined orange and lime juices over chicken and let marinate at least 30 minutes—an hour or two would be even better.

Meanwhile, cut lime rind into very thin strips about ½ inch (12 mm) long. Place them in a small saucepan with enough water to just cover and simmer about 5 minutes. Remove to a paper towel to drain, and reserve.

Preheat oven to 350°F. Bake chicken, covered, about 10 minutes, then turn the chicken over and bake uncovered another 10 to 15 minutes, or until juices run clear when chicken is pricked with a fork. Remove chicken to a serving platter and keep warm.

Liquid in bottom of pan should be almost gone and lightly browned. If not, return pan to oven and increase heat to 500°F. for a few minutes, watching carefully to make sure it doesn't burn. When juices have reduced to a tablespoon or two (15 to 30 ml), remove pan from oven and pour wine in immediately, scraping up browned bits from sides and bottom of pan. Pour this sauce over chicken and sprinkle with lime rind.

CHICKEN WITH
WATERCRESS-CREAM SAUCE

Watercress used to be more or less free for the taking wherever there were clean streams. Unpolluted streams are a rarity today and so is wild watercress, but watercress farming has become big business. Chinese cooks know the value of this dark green member of the nasturtium family, steaming or sautéing it to serve with seafood or meat. The French also use cresson *in any number of dishes. As a child, I used to pick off any sprigs used for garnish, having developed an early distrust of snippets of decorative food. But I was happy to eat watercress stewed in cream, puréed watercress blended with mashed potato, and of course, watercress soup. Serve this with Baked Tomatoes Stuffed with Kasha.*

Serves 4

1 whole chicken, 2½ to 3 pounds (1125 to 1350 g), cut in serving pieces	1 cup (250 ml) white wine
	1 bunch watercress
	1 shallot, minced
1 tablespoon (15 ml) sweet butter	1 cup (250 ml) whipping cream
1 tablespoon (15 ml) oil	Salt
1½ cups (375 ml) chicken broth	Pepper

Rinse chicken and pat dry. Cook it in a heavy skillet in butter and oil, turning frequently, until lightly browned (adjust heat as necessary). Pour in chicken broth and wine, cover skillet, and cook about 30 minutes, or until juices run clear, not pink, when drumstick is pierced with a fork.

Meanwhile, rinse watercress and discard tough stems. Place in a saucepan and steam over low heat, covered, about 3 minutes, or until watercress has wilted. When cool enough to handle, squeeze the moisture out of the watercress with your hands, then mince it finely with a sharp knife or in the food processor.

When chicken is done, arrange it in the center of a large, deep serving platter and keep it warm. Skim fat off the cooking juices. Add the shallot to the skillet and cook over high heat, stirring constantly, until juices have reduced to 3 to 4 tablespoons (30 to 45 ml). Stir in cream, salt, and pepper and cook over high heat another 3 minutes or so, until mixture has thickened slightly. Stir in watercress and pour in any juices that have accumulated under chicken. Cook for about 1 minute, then pour sauce around chicken and serve at once.

CHICKEN SHEPHERD'S PIE

No, no, not a timid shepherd—this is shepherd's pie made with poultry instead of the traditional lamb or beef, almost a chicken-potpie with potato crust. It's good, too. Serve it with Mushrooms Stuffed with Spinach and Pernod.

Traditional shepherd's pie is a sentimental favorite of mine because it was the first "grown-up" dish I learned to make when a college classmate gave me the recipe. She was the first of us to move into her own apartment, and one evening she invited a few friends over for shepherd's pie. Sitting at her tiny kitchen table in San Francisco, gossiping, and drinking Italian wine from straw-covered bottles, we all felt quite daring and sophisticated, a far cry from any shepherd heating his supper over a fire on a lonely hillside. But I'll bet our shepherd's pie tasted pretty much the same as his.

Serves 4 to 6

3 to 4 cups (750 to 1000 ml) cooked chicken, cut in bite-sized pieces

2 tablespoons (30 ml) sweet butter

1 tablespoon (15 ml) oil

2 medium leeks, sliced

2 medium stalks celery, sliced

5 to 6 medium mushrooms, sliced

2 medium carrots, sliced

1 cup (250 ml) chicken broth

½ cup (125 ml) white wine

3 tablespoons (45 ml) minced parsley

1 teaspoon (5 ml) fresh thyme, or ½ teaspoon (3 ml) dried

1 teaspoon (5 ml) minced fresh sage, or ½ teaspoon (3 ml) dried

1 teaspoon (5 ml) fresh marjoram leaves, or ½ teaspoon (3 ml) dried

1 small bay leaf

3 tablespoons (45 ml) butter
2 tablespoons (30 ml) flour
¼ cup (60 ml) milk
1 egg yolk
⅛ teaspoon (.5 ml) nutmeg
1 tablespoon (15 ml) lemon juice
Salt
Pepper

POTATO CRUST:

2 pounds (900 g) baking potatoes

5 tablespoons (75 ml) butter

¼ cup (60 ml) milk

Salt

Pepper
2 tablespoons (30 ml) grated Parmesan
Paprika

Check chicken to make sure all skin, fat, and bones have been removed. Reserve.

Heat 2 tablespoons (30 ml) butter and 1 tablespoon (15 ml) oil in a large skillet or casserole. Add leeks, celery, mushrooms, and carrots and cook, stirring, over medium heat for about 5 minutes. Add chicken broth, wine, and seasonings and simmer, covered, about 10 minutes, or until carrots are just tender. Discard bay leaf and remove vegetables with a slotted spoon to a bowl, reserving their cooking liquid.

In a saucepan, melt 3 tablespoons (45 ml) butter, then stir in flour. Pour in the vegetable cooking liquid and whisk over medium heat about 1 minute, or until beginning to thicken, then whisk in milk. Continue simmering another few minutes, or until mixture is as thick as light custard. Remove from heat and beat in egg yolk. Add nutmeg and lemon juice, and salt and pepper to taste. Combine mixture with vegetables and chicken and pour into a buttered 2-quart (2000-ml) baking dish.

To make potato crust, peel and quarter potatoes and cook them in boiling water about 20 minutes, or until tender. Mash them with a potato masher or force them through a foodmill or ricer, then beat 3 tablespoons (45 ml) of the butter, ¼ cup (60 ml) milk, salt, pepper and the Parmesan into them. Spread the potatoes smoothly over the top of the chicken mixture or pipe through a pastry bag fitted with a fluted tip. Melt the remaining 2 tablespoons (30 ml) butter and drizzle over the top of the crust. Sprinkle with paprika. Bake at 400°F. about 30 to 50 minutes, or until lightly browned on top, hot and bubbly inside.

ADVANCE PREPARATION: The entire pie may be assembled up to a day in advance and baked before serving (allow more baking time if the dish has just come out of the refrigerator).

COLD CHICKEN EN GELÉE

As a child I was fascinated by the cellophane-thin, almost transparent sheets of gelatin that our cook in France used to boil, strain, and clarify to make jellied dishes. I didn't actually like the taste, or at any rate the feel, of such gelatinous mixtures in those days, but I loved the way the dried sheets caught the light, like thinnest glass, and the magical way liquids were turned to jelly. I suppose this must have been isinglass, which I'm told is made from fish bladders. Knowing that, the whole process seems even more magical.

Cold chicken is standard summer fare. Serving it en gelée, *or jellied, makes an ordinary dish festive. Potato Salad with Radicchio and Green Bean Salad with Pesto would round out a cold supper nicely. Start with Cold Carrot Soup with Guacamole, and serve Chocolate Pudding with Praline for dessert.*

Serves 4 to 6

1 **whole chicken, about 5 pounds (2250 g), cut in serving pieces**	1 **tablespoon (15 ml) minced fresh tarragon, or ½ teaspoon (3 ml) dried**
2 **tablespoons (30 ml) oil**	**Salt**
1 **cup (250 ml) white wine**	2 **tablespoons (30 ml) minced fresh parsley**
2 **cups (500 ml) chicken broth**	1 **tablespoon (15 ml) gelatin**
1 **bay leaf**	⅓ **cup (85 ml) warm water**

GARNISH:

Few sprigs fresh tarragon or parsley	1 **bunch watercress**

Rinse chicken and pat dry. Separate the thigh from the leg if this hasn't been done already, and cut breast pieces in half so that they will fit more easily into the mold.

Cook chicken in oil over medium heat, turning frequently, until golden brown. Pour excess grease out of pan. Add wine, chicken broth, bay leaf, tarragon, salt, and parsley and simmer, uncovered, until chicken is tender, about 30 minutes. Remove bay leaf.

Place a few leaves fresh tarragon or parsley in the bottom of a ring mold, loaf pan, or bowl large enough to hold all the chicken. Arrange the pieces of chicken in the mold. Skim as much fat as possible from the broth. Dissolve gelatin in ⅓ cup (85 ml) warm water and stir it into the broth. Strain broth over the chicken. Refrigerate for several hours until it has jelled.

To serve, scrape all congealed fat off the surface. Invert onto a serving platter (give it a good shake if it resists unmolding). Garnish with watercress.

RABBIT IN WHITE WINE WITH FRESH SAGE

Americans have never cottoned to rabbit, so to speak, but our peasant ancestors certainly appreciated it whenever they could bag a wild hare. And rabbits were raised for the table on most small farms in Europe. Rabbit and hare are almost always stewed in wine—in fact, English jugged hare and French civet de lapin *are among the most classic country recipes. Add a handful of chopped fresh sage and serve the rabbit with Baked Polenta with Red Peppers. You'll wonder why more people don't eat rabbit.*

Serves 6

1 rabbit, 4 to 5 pounds (1800 to 2250 g), cut in serving pieces	1 bay leaf
	Salt
	Pepper
1 tablespoon (15 ml) oil	2 tablespoons (30 ml) tomato paste
3 tablespoons (45 ml) flour	
1 cup (250 ml) water	2 tablespoons (30 ml) whipping cream
2 cups (500 ml) white wine	
1 medium clove garlic	⅓ cup (85 ml) minced fresh sage leaves (see Note)
1 teaspoon (5 ml) fresh thyme, or ½ teaspoon (3 ml) dried	

NOTE: Dried sage can't be substituted for fresh here. If fresh is unavailable, simply follow the recipe without the herb.

Brown the rabbit pieces lightly in oil. Sprinkle flour over them and continue cooking another minute or two over medium heat. Pour in the water and wine and add the garlic, thyme, bay leaf, salt, and pepper. Stir in tomato paste. Simmer, covered, about 1½ hours, or until rabbit is very tender. Remove rabbit to serving platter and keep warm.

Stir in cream and cook sauce rapidly over high heat about 5 minutes, until it begins to thicken. Pour over rabbit and sprinkle minced sage over the top.

DUCK with PEARS

One of the most memorable Christmas Eves of my life was spent with friends in a small farmhouse in Brittany, where we feasted by the light of the tiny candles on the Christmas tree. The wind screeched in off the Atlantic and drummed on our windows, but we were warm and cozy inside as we proceeded to lap up dozens of icy oysters hauled from their beds a few hours earlier. We would certainly not have dreamed of venturing out into the gale, especially since an old blue-smocked man in the village had told us earlier that anyone foolish enough to be caught outside after dark might never be seen again. The prehistoric stone monuments in the area, the dolmens and menhirs, he explained, came to life on Christmas Eve. And any humans who happened to observe them dancing and swaying would be swallowed up and buried in the earth at their base—or at least that's what the paysans, the country people around here, believe, he said. We laughed at the story over dinner that evening, but secretly, I think, we all believed it ourselves, at least in that setting where Celtic ghosts competed with the holiday we were celebrating. Then one of the guests brought out two bottles of fine Chambertin (Napoleon's favorite wine, he told us). A platter of dark-skinned ducks surrounded by pears was brought in from the kitchen, and the conversation turned from ghost stories to more worldly matters.

Serve the duck with Sesame Spinach, and Potatoes with Garlic and Lemon Peel. Follow it with a wonderful dessert, such as Fresh Orange Cake with Bitter Chocolate Sauce—unless it's Christmas Eve, when you'll want a Christmas pudding.

Serves 4

1 **duck, 4 to 5 pounds (1800 to 2250 g), cut in 4 pieces**	1 **medium-sized ripe pear (Bosc or d'Anjou, for example)**
2 **tablespoons (30 ml) oil**	
1½ **cups (375 ml) white wine**	1 **tablespoon (15 ml) honey**

1 tablespoon (15 ml) grated
   gingerroot
2 tablespoons (30 ml)
   cornstarch

2 tablespoons (30 ml)
   brandy
   Salt
   Pepper

BAKED PEARS:

4 medium-sized ripe pears
2 tablespoons (30 ml) butter
2 tablespoons (30 ml) honey

¼ cup (60 ml) orange juice
1 tablespoon (15 ml) lemon
   juice

Prick duck all over with a fork so that fat can run out. Brown the pieces of duck in a heavy skillet, over medium heat, in the oil. Adjust heat as necessary to prevent scorching, and pour fat off occasionally.

Peel, quarter, and core one pear and purée it in a blender or food processor. When the duck has browned, remove it to a platter. Pour grease out of the skillet and add the puréed pear, wine, 1 tablespoon (15 ml) honey, and gingerroot. Bring to a boil, then simmer, stirring, about 2 minutes. Return duck to the skillet and spoon sauce over it. Reduce heat and simmer, covered, 45 to 50 minutes, or until duck is tender and cooked clear through. Remove duck to a serving platter.

Dissolve cornstarch in the brandy and stir it into the duck-cooking juices. Salt and pepper to taste. Simmer about 1 minute, or just until sauce begins to thicken. Pour sauce over duck and surround with the baked pears.

To make the pears, cut 4 pears in half and peel and core them. Place them in a buttered baking dish. In a saucepan, melt 2 tablespoons (30 ml) butter. Stir in 2 tablespoons (30 ml) honey, orange juice, and lemon juice. As soon as mixture is hot, pour over the pears. Bake 20 to 30 minutes, or until pears are tender, basting them occasionally.

MEATS

What say you to a piece of beef and mustard?

Shakespeare

Although many cultures have taboos about slaughtering and eating certain animals, most people in most parts of the world have been meat-eaters whenever they had the opportunity. Men were raising and eating giant oxen in Mesopotamia at least as far back as 2500 B.C. The Aztecs ate guinea pigs before cows were brought over by the Spaniards. A Chinese sage named I Yin wrote in 1500 B.C., "Of meat dishes the best are orang-utan lips . . . the tails of young swallows . . . and the choice parts of yak and elephant."

Whatever particular animal any given culture found tastiest, however, only the privileged classes consumed meat on a regular basis; most people throughout history subsisted on a diet that included very small amounts of meat on an occasional basis only. But as affluence spreads through a society, meat-eating increases—and so do coronary heart disease and other illnesses that are now believed to be at least partly related to overconsumption of meat and animal fats. According to recent surveys, health concerns prompted Americans to cut their red-meat consumption back from 57 pounds (25,650 g) per person in 1974 to 52 pounds (23,400 g) in 1982. Affluent Americans are beginning to eat in the manner of peasants, with meat in smaller portions, served less frequently.

Gone are the huge joints and haunches that our Victorian and Edwardian forebears feasted on. Gone too are the groaning boards laden with hams, sausages, roasts, and cutlets that were served forth at rural American celebrations in our grandparents' day. Few Americans dig into a big juicy steak on a regular basis these days, nor do we often have the time to prepare long-simmering stews.

Pass the stir-fried beef with fresh ginger and wild mushrooms.

Carbonnade in Brioches with Tenderloin of Beef

Lamb Tarts

Leg of Lamb with Pesto

Black Bean Chili con Carne

Beef Shanks with Fresh Plums and Ginger Sauce

Veal Paprikás

Chilled Meat Loaf with Chutney

Lamb Ragout with Fresh Vegetables

Gingered Pork with Cabbage

Ham Steaks with Spinach and Madeira

CARBONNADE IN BRIOCHES WITH TENDERLOIN OF BEEF

Carbonnade is a hearty beef and onion stew of Belgian origins. It is traditionally served with boiled potatoes, but in this version brioches—those rich rolls that usually have a topknot—are called for instead, and the meat and onions are cooked separately. Use homemade brioches or buy them in a bakery that carries French breads and pastries. A green vegetable would add a bright note to the meal: try Broccoli with Wasabi or Asparagus with Crème Fraîche and Chives.

Serves 4

1 small shallot, finely minced	1 12-ounce (372-ml) can beer
2 tablespoons (30 ml) oil	1½ cups (375 ml) beef stock
1 tablespoon (15 ml) soy sauce	1 teaspoon (5 ml) Dijon mustard
1 pound (450 g) beef tenderloin	Salt
	Pepper
4 medium onions, thinly sliced	1 tablespoon (15 ml) wine vinegar
2 medium cloves garlic, minced	4 brioches

Mix together the shallot, 1 tablespoon (15 ml) oil, and soy sauce and rub mixture into the meat. (If possible, do this several hours in advance and refrigerate.)

About 1½ hours before serving, cook the onions in remaining 1 tablespoon (15 ml) oil in a heavy kettle or casserole over medium–low heat, stirring frequently, until onions are limp and lightly colored, about 15 to 20 minutes. Add the garlic and cook another 5 minutes. Stir in the beer, beef stock, mustard, salt, pepper, and vinegar. Simmer, uncovered, over medium heat for 1 hour or until most of the liquid has cooked away.

About 30 minutes before serving, preheat the oven to 400°F. Place the tenderloin in a preheated oven for 15 to 20 minutes, depending on personal preference and thickness of beef.

Cut a small slice off the top of each brioche (about ½ inch [12 mm] plus the topknot that sits on traditional brioches). Pull out most of the inside of the brioches.

To serve, fill each of the brioche shells with the onion mixture and perch the tops back on them. Cut the beef into thin slices and arrange them next to the filled brioches.

ADVANCE PREPARATION: The onion mixture may be made a day or two ahead of time. If you're making your own brioches, they may be made a day or two in advance or up to 2 weeks ahead of time and frozen.

LAMB TARTS

*Mutton pies, steak and potato pasties, pork pies, beef and kidney pies—
all manner of meat pies have been made by British street vendors and home
cooks alike for centuries. In this fancier version of a rustic classic, tender lamb
slices nestle under individual filo crusts.*

*Buy half a lamb butt or other lamb roast and have the butcher cut out eight
slices for you, or do it yourself. The flavor of Parsley Root Purée is particularly well suited to this dish, but if parsley root isn't available, serve Glazed
Onions, along with Spinach with Garlic and Pine Nuts in Radicchio Cups.*

Serves 4

LAMB:

8 slices boneless lamb, about ½ inch (12 mm) thick, about 2 to 3 pounds (900 to 1350 g) total
1 tablespoon (15 ml) oil
¼ pound (112 g) mushrooms, sliced
1 teaspoon (5 ml) fresh thyme, or ½ teaspoon (3 ml) dried
½ teaspoon (3 ml) chili powder
Salt

CRUST:

4 sheets filo (see Note)
About ½ cup (125 ml) oil

NOTE: Comparing Middle Eastern filo (or phyllo) to pie crust is like
pointing out that butterflies and pigeons have something in common:
the first is light and delicate, the other seems stodgier, more earth-
bound. Filo sheets are usually bought ready-made, either fresh from
ethnic bakeries or frozen from the supermarket. Follow the simple
package directions for brushing each sheet with melted butter or oil,
making sure to keep the sheets you aren't actually working on covered
to keep them from drying out.

Place four of the lamb slices on a lightly oiled baking sheet. Cook
the mushrooms in 1 tablespoon (15 ml) oil over medium-low heat
until they are limp. Stir in thyme, chili powder, and salt. Divide
mushroom mixture among the four lamb slices, spreading the mixture
over each one. Top each with another slice of lamb.

To make the crust, brush oil over each sheet of filo. Stack the four
sheets together and fold stack in half. Cut in quarters. Drape each
quarter over the top of the lamb pieces.

About 40 minutes before serving, preheat the oven to 425°F. Bake the lamb pies about 20 minutes, or until meat is done to your taste and crust has browned.

LEG of LAMB with PESTO

Lamb has been associated with spring celebrations since the beginning of history. Thanks to modern animal husbandry and refrigeration, we can now enjoy lamb all year round.

Ask the butcher to bone and butterfly the leg of lamb for you. Lima Bean Purée with Rosemary and Buttermilk goes well with this, and you might want to start the meal with Rutabaga-Tomato Soup.

Serves 6 to 8

1 leg of lamb, 6 to 7 pounds (2700 to 3150 g), boned and butterflied

4 to 5 cups (1000 to 1250 ml) fresh basil leaves

3 large cloves garlic, chopped

⅓ cup (85 ml) pine nuts

1 cup (250 ml) olive oil

Salt

Pepper

Lay the meat, skin side down, on a flat surface.

Place basil, garlic, and half the pine nuts in a blender or food processor. Turn machine on and off several times, scraping down the sides if necessary, until mixture is finely chopped. With the machine running, pour in the oil in a thin stream. Add salt and pepper to taste. Spread about a third of this pesto mixture on the surface of the lamb, reserving the rest. Sprinkle the remaining pine nuts over it. Roll the lamb into a compact cylindrical shape, skewering it together if necessary. Tie loops of string around it at 1-inch (25-mm) intervals to hold the meat in shape. Salt and pepper the outside of the roast if you wish.

Place roast in a preheated 450°F. oven. Cook for 15 to 20 minutes, or until surface is lightly browned, then turn oven down to 350°F. Continue cooking about 1½ hours for medium-rare (juices will run rosy when roast is pricked with a fork), 1 hour and 45 minutes for well done (juices run yellow).

Let the roast sit about 10 minutes after it comes out of the oven. Spread reserved pesto around the bottom of a warmed serving platter. Carve the lamb into slices and arrange them on top of the pesto.

ADVANCE PREPARATION: The lamb may be spread with pesto, rolled, and tied several hours in advance.

BLACK BEAN CHILI CON CARNE

Although chili con carne is usually made with pink, pinto, or red kidney beans, why not use black beans instead? After all, Mexicans were eating black beans 7,000 years ago, so they've certainly stood the test of time. Black beans give the dish a rich flavor and deep color that provides a beautiful background for a splash of lime-flecked sour cream. If you like dumplings, try the Corn Dumpling garnish, or serve the chili with Baked Polenta with Red Peppers. A plain green salad or Leaf Lettuce with Cayenned Walnuts would round the meal out nicely.

Serves 6 to 8

1 large onion, minced
3 medium cloves garlic, minced
1 pound (450 g) lean ground beef (see Note)
3 tablespoons (45 ml) chili powder
1 teaspoon (5 ml) cumin
1 teaspoon (5 ml) oregano
1 teaspoon (5 ml) red pepper flakes

2 16-ounce (500 ml) cans tomato purée
2 cups (500 ml) coarsely chopped tomatoes, fresh or canned
1 cup (250 ml) red or white wine
4 cups (1000 ml) cooked black beans
Salt

GARNISH:
1 cup (250 ml) sour cream
Grated rind of 1 lime

Corn Dumplings (recipe follows), optional

NOTE: Add another pound (450 g) of meat if you like your chili meaty.

Cook onion and garlic along with meat in a sturdy kettle or casserole over medium-high heat, stirring frequently (you won't need oil if the kettle is heavy enough). When the meat has colored and onions are soft, stir in seasonings. Add tomato purée and chopped tomatoes, wine, and beans. Simmer, uncovered, about 1½ hours. Stir frequently to prevent scorching. Adjust seasoning to taste. Prepare

Corn Dumplings, if desired, and serve chili and dumplings topped with sour cream sprinkled with lime rind.

ADVANCE PREPARATION: Chili is always best made a day or two ahead of time. Refrigerate it for up to 4 days, or freeze for several weeks.

CORN DUMPLINGS

1 cup (250 ml) corn kernels
1 cup (250 ml) unbleached flour
1 teaspoon (5 ml) baking powder
3 tablespoons (45 ml) yellow or white cornmeal
1 egg
⅓ cup (85 ml) milk
Salt

Place corn, flour, baking powder, cornmeal, egg, milk, and salt in food processor or blender and process until smooth. Drop by spoonfuls into simmering chili, cover tightly, and cook 15 minutes without removing the cover.

BEEF SHANKS with FRESH PLUMS and GINGER SAUCE

Fresh fruit rounds out flavors and adds an appealing piquancy to stewed meats, a fact that peasant cultures around the world are well aware of. A Russian tradition blends meat or chicken in a stewpot with fresh plums; South Americans make carbonada criolla, *or beef stew with peaches; Middle Eastern cuisine favors lamb stewed with apricots; and the French like rabbit stewed with prunes.*

Red-fleshed plums add the best color to this dish, but if they are unavailable use whatever fresh plums you can get. Serve the beef shanks with Barley-Leek Gratin or Black-eyed Peas with Garlic and Parsley and Fondant of Swiss Chard with Cream.

Serves 4 to 6

3½ to 4 pounds (1575 to 1800 g) beef shanks
2 teaspoons (30 ml) oil
1 medium onion, cut in quarters
1 carrot, sliced
3 medium cloves garlic, chopped
½ teaspoon (3 ml) thyme
½ teaspoon (3 ml) marjoram

2 cups (500 ml) beef stock
1 cup (250 ml) white wine
4 fresh plums, about 1
   pound (450 g)
2 tablespoons (30 ml)
   minced gingerroot

½ teaspoon (3 ml) red
   pepper flakes
Salt
Pepper

In a casserole, brown the beef shanks in oil over medium-high heat. Add the onion, carrot, garlic, thyme, and marjoram and continue cooking 3 to 4 minutes, until the onion begins to color. Pour in the beef stock and the wine and simmer, uncovered, about 1½ hours, or until the meat is very tender. Remove the shanks from the cooking broth and reserve them.

Cut the plums in quarters and add them to the casserole. Add the ginger, pepper flakes, salt, and pepper. Simmer, uncovered, about 15 minutes, or until plums are tender. Transfer sauce to food processor or blender (in batches if necessary) and purée it. Return it to the casserole and cook over high heat, uncovered, about 10 minutes, or until reduced by about a third. Return meat to the casserole and reheat it.

ADVANCE PREPARATION: The entire dish may be made up to a day ahead of time.

VEAL PAPRIKÁS

One man yearns for fame, another for wealth, but everyone yearns for paprika goulash.

Hungarian proverb

Before 1492 many Europeans may have yearned for fame or wealth, but paprika, a native of the American continent, was as yet unknown to them. A member of the genus Capsicum, *paprika comes from a pepper whose level of intensity is mild rather than wild (chili powder is made from a hotter member of this same family). In addition to its appealing fragrance and vivid color, paprika is a rich source of vitamin C.*

You could substitute chicken breasts for the veal if you wish. Serve this dish with noodles as they do in Hungary, or with Barley-Leek Gratin.

Serves 4

4 veal scallops (or 2 large boneless, skinless chicken breasts, halved), about 1½ pounds (675 g) total
1 tablespoon (15 ml) sweet butter
1 medium shallot, minced
¼ pound (112 g) mushrooms, sliced
1 teaspoon (3 ml) paprika

1 teaspoon (3 ml) chile powder
½ cup (125 ml) chicken stock
½ cup white wine
⅓ cup (85 ml) Crème Fraîche (see Cornmeal Crêpes with Crème Fraîche and Caviar for recipe) or sour cream

Pound the veal or chicken with a meat mallet or the edge of a saucer until it is no more than ¼ inch (6 mm) thick. Cook the meat in butter in a skillet over medium-low heat until it has just lost its pink color, turning once. When done, remove to a plate and keep warm. Add the shallot and mushrooms to the pan and cook, stirring frequently, over medium heat until shallots are soft (add a little more butter or some oil if necessary). Stir in paprika and chili powder. Add wine and chicken stock and raise heat to high. Cook for about 5 minutes. Reduce heat to low. Stir in Crème Fraîche or sour cream. Return meat to pan just long enough to reheat. Serve immediately.

CHILLED MEAT LOAF WITH CHUTNEY

I've found that the humble meat loaf, served cold and weighted down to give it a dense texture like a French pâté, is an exceptionally successful party dish. To serve a large group I usually make three or four meat loaves and offer a selection of chutneys to go with them. For a summer party or picnic, serve the meat loaf with large bowls of Potato Salad with Radicchio and Papaya, Red Onion, and Apple Salad, with Pears Baked with Cassis for dessert.

Serves 6

2 pounds (900 g) ground beef
1 pound (450 g) ground pork
2 medium cloves garlic, minced

1 large onion, minced
1 teaspoon (3 ml) dried thyme
1 teaspoon (3 ml) dried rosemary

½ cup (125 ml) bread
crumbs
2 eggs, beaten

Salt
Pepper

GARNISH:
Mango or other fruit chutney

Preheat oven to 350°F. Mix all ingredients together. Pack mixture into an ungreased loaf pan and bake at 350°F. for 1 to 1½ hours, or until meat loaf is done clear through. Drain off all the grease. When meat loaf has cooled, cover with foil and place a brick or cans of food or another heavy object on top of it and refrigerate several hours or overnight.

To serve, remove meat loaf from pan and slice. Serve accompanied by chutney.

ADVANCE PREPARATION: Make meat loaf at least one day in advance for flavors to meld. Can be made up to two days in advance.

LAMB RAGOUT WITH FRESH VEGETABLES

Contemporary stews and ragouts are no longer thickened with flour but with puréed fresh vegetables. Add the smallest, freshest vegetables you can find: tiny zucchini or other squashes, baby eggplant if possible, little new potatoes. Serve the ragout over Baked Polenta with Red Peppers if you wish, accompanied by a green salad. Walnut Bread Pudding with Apricot Rum Sauce would be a good dessert.

Serves 6 to 8

3 to 4 pounds (1350 to 1800 g) boneless leg of lamb, trimmed of fat and cut in bite-sized pieces

2 tablespoons (30 ml) olive oil

4 large carrots, about ½ pound (225 g) total

2 medium onions, peeled and cut in half

3 whole large cloves garlic, peeled

3 medium tomatoes, peeled and seeded

2 teaspoons (10 ml) fresh rosemary, or 1 teaspoon (5 ml) dried

1 tablespoon (15 ml) fresh thyme, or 1 teaspoon (5 ml) dried

¼ cup (60 ml) chopped
    parsley
5 cups (1250 ml) chicken
    stock

2 teaspoons (30 ml) tomato
    paste
Salt
Pepper

VEGETABLES—SELECT A VARIETY FROM AMONG:

New potatoes
Baby carrots
Snow peas
Small green beans

Zucchini or yellow squash
Whole baby corn cobs
Pearl onions

Cook the lamb in olive oil over medium-high heat until lightly browned. Cut the 4 large carrots in 1-inch (25-mm) chunks and add to meat along with onion halves, garlic cloves, tomatoes, rosemary, thyme, parsley, chicken stock, and tomato paste. Simmer, covered, for about an hour, or until lamb is tender. Remove lamb with a slotted spoon and reserve. Transfer cooked vegetables to a food processor or blender and purée them. Return to the kettle along with the meat. About 20 minutes before serving, add the whole new potatoes, pearl onions, and any other vegetables that take a relatively long time to cook and simmer them until tender. Five to ten minutes before serving, add snow peas, green beans, zucchini (sliced if not very tiny), and other vegetables that cook quickly. Add salt and pepper. The vegetables should be simmered until tender but not mushy.

GINGERED PORK with CABBAGE

Pork—because it is relatively inexpensive, and pigs are simple to raise —is the most commonly eaten meat in the world. Few peasants take their good fortune lightly. In France, for example, farmers have traditionally called their pigs "monsieur," as a token of the respect they feel for this useful animal. I was once told a story about a farmer near Toulouse who, when the Germans were commandeering provisions, wrapped his pig in baby blankets, tied him down in a carriage, and succeeded in passing "monsieur" off as his last-born son.

Serve this dish with Baked Tomatoes Stuffed with Kasha, or Carrots with Honey and Fresh Mint.

Serves 4

About 1 pound (450 g) boneless pork loin or tenderloin
2 medium cloves garlic, minced
2 tablespoons (30 ml) finely minced gingerroot
6 green onions, sliced

¼ cup (60 ml) soy sauce
¼ cup (60 ml) white wine
½ teaspoon (3 ml) dried red pepper flakes
1 small head cabbage, 1 to 1 ½ pounds (450 to 675 g)
1 tablespoon (15 ml) oil

Trim off any fat and slice pork into thin strips about 1 × ¼ inch (25 × 6 mm). In a bowl, toss the meat along with garlic, gingerroot, green onions, soy sauce, wine, and pepper flakes. Let marinate at least 10 minutes.

Shred cabbage with a sharp knife. Heat oil for a few seconds in a wok or large heavy skillet. Remove pork from marinade with a slotted spoon, reserving marinade. Cook pork over high heat, stirring constantly, about 4 or 5 minutes, or until all trace of pink is gone (cut a piece in half to check). Remove meat from pan and add the cabbage. Stir to coat with pan juices, then lower heat and simmer, covered, about 5 minutes, or until cabbage is tender but still has some crunch to it. Return pork to pan, pour in marinade, and toss for a few seconds.

HAM STEAKS WITH SPINACH AND MADEIRA

I have a friend who, like many Manhattan residents, would often escape from urban tensions to a small house in the country. Here she attempted to discover her peasant roots by raising vegetables, berries, two goats, and a pig named Ethel. One memorable Sunday morning my friend and her houseful of guests from New York woke to find that Ethel and the goats had escaped from their pen, ripped out all the rosebushes, and eaten most of the screen door leading to the kitchen. The goats were standing in the road tying up traffic, while Ethel was lying contentedly on the rug in front of the fireplace, waiting for breakfast. A photograph of her in this position dominated the table when I attended an Ethel-ham dinner some months later.

Potatoes go well with this. Try Potato-Mushroom Gratin or Potatoes with Garlic and Lemon Peel.

Serves 4

1 or 2 ham steaks about ¾ inch (18 mm) thick, 2 pounds (900 g) total
2 tablespoons (30 ml) sweet butter

½ cup (125 ml) Madeira
2 pounds (900 g) spinach

Trim excess fat from ham and cook the steaks in butter in a heavy skillet, turning a couple of times. When they are lightly browned, pour in half the Madeira and cook over high heat a minute or two, until the wine has almost disappeared. Turn ham slices over and remove skillet from heat for about 5 minutes to allow meat to absorb juices.

Meanwhile, trim and rinse spinach and cook it in a large covered kettle, in only the water clinging to its leaves, for 3 to 5 minutes, or until it has wilted. Drain thoroughly, squeezing out excess water.

Return ham to stove and cook over medium heat until warm clear through. Remove ham and pour remaining Madeira in skillet. Cook for a minute, swirling the pan lightly. Add spinach and toss briefly to reheat and coat with the pan juices. Mound spinach on a serving platter and arrange the ham on top.

PASTA, BEANS, AND OTHER LIGHT MAIN DISHES

Pease porridge hot, pease porridge cold,
Pease porridge in the pot, nine days old.

Old English rhyme

Peas, lentils, pasta, and other legumes and grain-based foods have become popular in our society because of the recently emphasized contribution of these complex carbohydrates to human health. But for the peasant, foods of this type were indeed the traditional staff of life. Bread of one kind or another was all too often the only food available to nourish an impoverished peasantry, from ancient Egypt through classical and medieval Europe.

Even during periods free of famine, the world's peasants subsisted largely on gruels, puddings, and porridges whose main ingredients were grains or legumes. Peas, which probably originated in Asia, were valuable in peasant diets the world over, primarily in dried form. Like dried beans and lentils, dried peas could be preserved practically forever raw and, as the pease-porridge rhyme indicates, kept around a good long time even after they were cooked. Corn, which could also be dried, was the foundation of the Aztec diet, in the form of corn tortillas supplemented by bean stews and corn porridges. When corn was introduced to Africa by the Portuguese it became a staple there. Buckwheat, a native of Asia, became a favorite food in Eastern Europe, where it is sometimes called kasha. Lentils, whose provenance is unknown, are a peasant staple the world over (lentil stew is surely the "mess of pottage" for which Esau sold his birthright.) Rice, probably indigenous to India, is still the central food for millions of people in Asia, second only to wheat in worldwide importance. Wheat, which was probably first cultivated in Mesopotamia, is now the most widely distributed cereal in the world; in addition to its main use in bread, wheat also served to make such things as medieval English frumenty, a sweet, puddinglike dish.

A variety of wheat called durum is the central ingredient in most pasta. Pasta has a long history that begins, probably, in China, arrives in Italy long before Marco Polo's travels, sustains generations of European peasants (noodles in Britain, *spaetzle* in Austria, *nouilles* in France), and ends up the most popular item on elegant American dinner menus today.

Linguine with Shrimp and Fresh Ginger

Black-eyed Peas with Garlic and Parsley

Rice with Black-eyed Peas and Sun-dried Tomatoes

Wild Mushroom Ragout

Baked Polenta with Red Peppers

Black Bean Cakes

Baked Ziti with Smoked Salmon and Sun-dried Tomatoes

Tortellini in Brodo with Swiss Chard and Red Pepper

Zucchini Tian with Goat Cheese

Barley-Leek Gratin

Chicken Liver Soufflé with Fresh Tomato Sauce

Brown Rice Pilau

Black Beans and Rice with Oranges and Onion Sauce

Lasagne with Chicken and Marsala

LINGUINE WITH SHRIMP AND FRESH GINGER

Shrimp get around, perhaps because they have ten legs. You'll find several species in the Atlantic, a few in the Pacific, and still others in the Caribbean. You can imagine how many peasant cooking pots they've turned up in around the world! Try cooking them with fresh ginger—after all, according to an Indian proverb, "Every good quality is found in ginger."

Serves 4 to 6

1 shallot, minced
¼ cup (60 ml) oil
2 medium cloves garlic, minced
1 tablespoon (15 ml) soy sauce
½ cup chicken stock
⅛ teaspoon (.5 ml) cayenne pepper

2 tablespoons (30 ml) finely minced gingerroot
1 pound (450 g) cooked and shelled shrimp
1 pound (450 g) homemade or commercial linguine

Cook shallot in oil until soft. Add the garlic and cook another 30 seconds. Add the soy sauce, chicken stock, cayenne, and gingerroot and simmer about 2 minutes. Just before serving, add the shrimp and simmer just long enough to heat the shrimp through.

Cook linguine al dente, until it is just tender. Toss with the shrimp mixture and serve at once.

ADVANCE PREPARATION: You could cook the shallot with the garlic, soy sauce, stock, cayenne, and gingerroot several hours in advance. Reheat at the last minute and add shrimp.

BLACK-EYED PEAS WITH GARLIC AND PARSLEY

Like many other American soul-food specialties, black-eyed peas, which are Asian natives, came to the United States from Africa along with the slave trade.

Serve this dish with Scallops with Braised Fennel, or with meat or poultry. Or serve it mixed with oil and vinegar as a salad—this is known as Texas caviar. Leftovers may be mixed with rice to make Rice with Black-eyed Peas and Sun-dried Tomatoes.

Serves 6 to 8

1 pound (450 g) dried black-eyed peas	Salt
	Pepper
6 cups (1500 ml) water	½ cup (125 ml) olive oil
1 medium onion, whole	2 large cloves garlic, minced
1 bay leaf	¼ cup (60 ml) minced parsley
1 teaspoon (5 ml) dried thyme, or 1 tablespoon (15 ml) fresh thyme	

Place peas in a sieve and rinse under cold water, picking through them to remove any bits of dirt or gravel. Put them in a kettle with 6 cups (1500 ml) water, onion, bay leaf, and thyme. Simmer, partially covered, 30 to 40 minutes, or until peas are tender. Add salt and pepper. Drain well, discarding onion and bay leaf.

Mix together olive oil, garlic, and parsley. Pour over peas and toss. Serve hot or cold.

RICE WITH BLACK-EYED PEAS AND SUN-DRIED TOMATOES

In Louisiana they eat red beans and rice, in Cuba it's black beans with rice (called moros y cristianos, *or Moors and Christians). Venetians mix rice and peas and call it* risi i bisi, *while Indonesian* gado-gado *combines rice with another legume, peanuts. The combination of rice and legumes makes sense nutritionally as well as gastronomically since each supplies an amino acid the other lacks, forming a complete protein when they are united.*

Serve this dish as a main course accompanied by Spinach with Garlic and Pine Nuts in Radicchio Cups or Carrot Tart with Spinach "Crust" and a green salad. Or serve it as a side dish with meat or poultry dishes.

Serves 6 to 8

2 cups (500 ml) cooked black-eyed peas (1 cup uncooked)	2 ounces (60 ml) oil-packed sun-dried tomatoes, drained
2 cups (500 ml) cooked rice (⅔ cup [170 ml] uncooked)	Salt Pepper

Combine black-eyed peas and rice. Cut tomatoes into pieces about an inch (25 mm) long. Mix all ingredients together, including 2 or 3 tablespoons [30 to 45 ml] oil from the tomatoes if possible. Season with salt and pepper. Pack mixture into a greased soufflé mold or other decorative baking dish. Cover and bake at 350°F. for about 30 minutes, or until hot clear through.

ADVANCE PREPARATION: Ingredients may be combined up to a day ahead of time and refrigerated until ready to bake.

WILD MUSHROOM RAGOUT

Peasants in Asia who could rarely afford meat ate wild mushrooms instead. American researchers studying Chinese and Japanese diets now suspect that properties in some of these mushrooms may help prevent heart disease and some forms of cancer as well as stimulate the immune system. It's good to know that we may be prolonging our lives as well as enriching our gastronomic experience by becoming familiar with some of the exotic mushrooms that are appearing more and more in American markets. If you've got a terrific greengrocer, you may be able to choose from among a selection of fresh cèpes, shiitake (sometimes called dubloons), oyster, enoki, morel, or chanterelle mushrooms. Serve this as a first course, as an accompaniment to plain roast meat or chicken, or as a main course accompanied by rice or Baked Polenta with Red Peppers.

Serves 4 to 6

1 tablespoon (15 ml) olive oil

1 tablespoon (15 ml) sweet butter

1 slice blanched bacon (optional, see Note)

1 medium shallot, minced

1 medium onion, minced

1 carrot, thinly sliced

¾ to 1 pound (336 to 450 g) assorted fresh wild mushrooms

1 tablespoon (15 ml) flour

⅔ cup (170 ml) chicken stock

⅔ cup (170 ml) red wine

2 teaspoons (30 ml) fresh thyme, or ½ teaspoon (3 ml) dried

Salt

Pepper

NOTE: To blanch bacon, simmer it in enough water to cover for about 3 minutes. Drain and rinse with cold water.

In a heavy skillet or casserole, heat oil and butter over medium heat until butter melts. Mince the bacon and add it to the skillet along with shallot, onion, and carrot. Cook for about 5 minutes, stirring frequently, until onion is limp and translucent.

Wipe mushrooms clean. Slice them thickly and add to the skillet. Stir them over low heat for a minute or two. Sprinkle with flour and continue cooking, stirring constantly, another minute. Pour in chicken stock and wine. Add thyme, salt, and pepper. Simmer, covered, about 20 minutes.

ADVANCE PREPARATION: The dish may be made up to a day ahead of time and reheated.

BAKED POLENTA with RED PEPPERS

Like some people, certain foods travel around the world, settling sometimes in a foreign country where they become more native than the real natives. Corn is just such an example: arriving in Italy from America in the sixteenth century, it was promptly converted into a sort of cornmeal mush called polenta, which became one of the staples of Italy's cucina paisana.

Serve this simplified polenta in slices, with Wild Mushroom Ragout or Leg of Lamb with Pesto. For a richer dish, sauté the slices in butter (see Variation).

Serves 4

½ cup (125 ml) yellow
cornmeal
½ cup (125 ml) cold water
2 cups (500 ml) boiling
water

Salt
2 tablespoons (30 ml)
minced red bell pepper
2 tablespoons (30 ml) grated
Parmesan

Mix cornmeal and ½ cup (125 ml) cold water in the top of a double
boiler. Gradually pour in 2 cups (500 ml) boiling water, stirring
constantly. Add salt to taste. Simmer, covered, over boiling water for
about 15 minutes, stirring frequently. Remove from heat and stir in
red pepper. Pour mixture into a generously oiled loaf pan. Sprinkle
Parmesan over the top and bake at 375°F. for about 40 minutes, or until
browned on top. Turn it out on a platter and cut in slices.

VARIATION: Before serving, slice polenta and sauté slices in 2 tablespoons (30 ml) butter, turning once, until browned on both sides.

ADVANCE PREPARATION: Polenta may be made up to 2 days in
advance and baked or reheated before serving. Or for the Variation,
bake it ahead of time, then sauté slices in butter before serving.

BLACK BEAN CAKES

---

*Dried beans have kept peasant civilizations alive across the globe, from
ancient Sumerians and Aztecs to medieval Europeans and Colonial Americans. Because their fairly bland flavor enables them to absorb flavors readily,
beans adapt deliciously to almost any ethnic cuisine.*

*These bean cakes may be served as a first course (garnish with avocado
slices or guacamole, if you wish, in addition to the sour cream and lime) or
as an accompaniment to simple meat or chicken dishes. Or serve them as a
main course, along with Papaya, Red Onion, and Apple Salad.*

Makes about 12 bean cakes

1 pound (450 g) dried black
beans
6 cups (1500 ml) water
1 onion, peeled and cut in
half
5 medium cloves garlic,
whole, peeled

1 bay leaf
1 teaspoon (5 ml) dried
oregano
½ teaspoon (3 ml) red
pepper flakes
2 tablespoons (30 ml) flour
Olive oil

¼ pound (112 g) California
  chiles, charred, peeled, and
  chopped, or 1 4-ounce
  (125-ml) can whole or
  chopped green chiles

GARNISH:
  2 limes, cut into wedges
  2 cups (500 ml) sour cream
    (see Note)

NOTE: For a lower-calorie dish, substitute yogurt for sour cream or stir 1 cup (250 ml) yogurt into 1 cup (250 ml) sour cream.

Rinse beans and place them in a large kettle along with water, onion, garlic, bay leaf, oregano, and red pepper flakes. Bring to a boil and simmer, partially covered, about 1½ to 2 hours, or until beans are very tender. Discard bay leaf and onion. Drain beans thoroughly and transfer to a blender or food processor. Add flour. Turn machine on and off several times to mash beans coarsely without turning them into an absolutely smooth purée. If chiles are not already chopped, mince them and stir into bean mixture.

Generously oil two baking sheets. Form bean mixture into patties about the size of hamburgers (it will be easier to work with if you grease the palms of your hands lightly with olive oil). Arrange patties on greased baking sheets.

Preheat oven to 400°F. Drizzle a little olive oil over the bean cakes. Bake them about 20 to 25 minutes, or until thoroughly warmed and beginning to get a little crusty on top (it is not necessary to turn them). With a spatula, carefully transfer bean cakes to individual serving plates. Garnish with lime wedges and pass a bowl of sour cream separately.

BAKED ZITI with SMOKED SALMON and SUN-DRIED TOMATOES

Pasta, of course, is the national dish of Italy. Although it has become popular in the United States, Italians still consume six times as much pasta as we do. Recent studies show that Italians suffer significantly less heart disease than their American peers, perhaps in part because their diet is high in pasta's nutritious complex carbohydrates.

110

Serve this with Mâche with Warm Shiitake Mushrooms as a first course, and follow with a spectacular dessert—Orange Cake with Bitter Chocolate Sauce, for example.

Serves 4

1 pound (450 g) cooked ziti
3 tablespoons (45 ml) sweet butter
15 ounces (420 g) ricotta cheese
¼ pound (112 g) smoked salmon
8 to 10 ounces (250 to 310 ml) oil-packed sun-dried tomatoes, drained

1 cup (250 ml) whipping cream
1 bay leaf
¼ cup (60 ml) vodka
½ cup (125 ml) fresh bread crumbs

Spread a third of the ziti in a baking dish that has been greased with 1 tablespoon (15 ml) of the butter. Top with half the ricotta. Cut the salmon and tomatoes into bite-sized pieces and scatter half of them over the ricotta (include any oil from the tomatoes). Cover with half the remaining ziti and all of the remaining ricotta, salmon, and tomatoes. Add the remaining ziti.

Place heavy cream, bay leaf, and vodka in a saucepan. Simmer for about 5 minutes, or until slightly reduced and thick enough to coat the back of a spoon. Pour over ziti. Distribute bread crumbs over top and dot with remaining butter. Bake, covered, at 350°F. for 15 minutes. Remove cover and continue baking about 20 minutes more, or until mixture is hot and bubbly.

ADVANCE PREPARATION: Pasta, ricotta, salmon, and tomatoes may be arranged in baking dish 1 or 2 hours ahead of time, and sauce may be reduced. Before serving, reheat sauce, pour over pasta, and bake.

TORTELLINI IN BRODO WITH SWISS CHARD AND RED PEPPER

Generations of Italians have found steaming bowls of tortellini in broth the best way to take the chill off a rural winter evening.
Use tortellini stuffed with cheese, veal, spinach, or porcini mushrooms. In

season, you could substitute broccoli rabe or any other fresh leafy green for the Swiss chard.

Serves 4

1 pound (450 g) tortellini
1 cup (250 ml) chicken stock
5 cups (1250 ml) shredded Swiss chard leaves (about 1 bunch chard)
1 red pepper, cut in strips (see Note)
1 tablespoon (15 ml) minced fresh basil, or 1 teaspoon (5 ml) dried
½ teaspoon (3 ml) dried oregano
½ teaspoon (3 ml) dried red pepper flakes
1 tablespoon (15 ml) sour cream
2 teaspoons (10 ml) soy sauce
Salt
Freshly ground black pepper
Grated Parmesan

NOTE: Use roasted peppers if you prefer. Buy them water- or oil-packed, or make your own by broiling a red pepper until it is black and blistered. Place it in a plastic or paper bag until cool enough to handle, then pull off the peel. Remove stem, seeds, and membrane and cut pepper in strips.

Cook tortellini until just tender, about 12 minutes depending on size. Drain.

Meanwhile, bring chicken stock to a boil. Stir in Swiss chard. Simmer, stirring occasionally, 2 or 3 minutes, or until chard wilts. Stir in remaining ingredients except Parmesan. Add tortellini and ladle into four individual serving bowls. Pass Parmesan separately.

ZUCCHINI TIAN with GOAT CHEESE

A tian *is a large earthenware baking dish used in Provence, and anything baked in it is also apt to be called a* tian. *Zucchini, spinach, or Swiss chard is typically used, and a cup or two of cooked rice is often stirred into the mixture.* Tians *are a staple of country cooking in Provence and are often eaten cold on picnics. This may be served as an accompaniment to meat or chicken or as a main course: start with Crab Chowder with Crème Fraîche and Lime, then serve the* tian *with Tomatoes with Balsamic Vinegar and Shallots, and Scalloped Onions.*

Serves 4 to 6

4 medium zucchini,
  shredded, about 2 cups
  (500 ml)
3 eggs
  About 4 ounces (112 g)
  soft goat cheese, such as

Montrachet
5 green onions, sliced
Salt
3 tablespoons (45 ml) grated
  Parmesan
Olive oil

Place shredded zucchini in a colander or strainer set over a bowl and let drain for about 10 minutes, giving it a squeeze from time to time to extract juices.

Preheat oven to 375°F. Beat eggs and stir them together with goat cheese, green onions, zucchini, and salt. Pour mixture into a buttered earthenware or other baking dish, sprinkle with Parmesan, and drizzle a little olive oil over the top. Bake at 375°F. about 45 to 60 minutes, or until bubbly and lightly browned on top. Serve hot, at room temperature, or cold.

BARLEY-LEEK GRATIN

It is a mystery to me why Americans think barley is something whose sole purpose in life is to keep beef company in soup. In fact, this excellent grain is as simple to cook as rice, reheats easily, and its mild flavor and slightly chewy texture make it the ideal companion for all sorts of dishes. It's an excellent buffet party dish since it can be made well ahead of time and doesn't mind sitting around a buffet table. Try it with Deep-dish Drumstick Pie, Beef Shanks with Fresh Plums and Ginger Sauce, or Fish Mousse with Lobster and Saffron Cream Sauce.

Serves 8 to 10

1 large onion, minced
2 medium cloves garlic,
  minced
1 carrot, thinly sliced
2 tablespoons (30 ml) oil
1 bunch leeks (about 3
  leeks)
2 cups (1 pound [450 g])
  raw barley

½ teaspoon (3 ml) dried
  thyme
Salt
Pepper
6 cups (1500 ml) water or
  chicken stock
2 tablespoons (30 ml) grated
  Parmesan

Cook onion, garlic, and carrot in oil over medium-low heat until onion softens.

Cut off about 2 inches (50 mm) from the tough green top of the leeks and discard. Trim off roots. Cut leeks in half lengthwise and rinse carefully to get rid of all sand and grit. Slice the leeks and stir them into the onion mixture along with the barley. Add thyme, salt, and pepper and cook for about 5 minutes. Pour in water or chicken stock.

Transfer mixture to a decorative baking dish and bake, covered, at 350°F. for about 40 minutes, or until all liquid is absorbed and barley is soft. Remove cover, sprinkle barley with Parmesan, turn oven up to 425°F., and continue baking another 5 minutes or so, until cheese has melted and browned lightly.

ADVANCE PREPARATION: Dish may be prepared up to 3 days ahead of time and refrigerated, or up to 2 weeks in advance and frozen. Reheat in the oven.

CHICKEN LIVER SOUFFLÉ
WITH FRESH TOMATO SAUCE

I like the way an airy, delicate soufflé mixture harmonizes with something as sturdy-flavored as chicken livers. Serve this for brunch or as a light supper. Or bake the mixture in individual ramekins to be unmolded and served as a first course. You might want to follow it with Roast Chicken with Garlic and Fresh Ginger, and a simple green vegetable such as Sesame Spinach.

Serves

½ pound (225 g) chicken livers

1 small onion, minced

4 tablespoons (60 ml) sweet butter

2 tablespoons (30 ml) flour

¼ cup (60 ml) Cognac

1 tablespoon (15 ml) minced fresh basil, or 1 teaspoon (5 ml) dried

1 tablespoon (15 ml) fresh tarragon, or ½ teaspoon (5 ml) dried

2 tablespoons (30 ml) minced parsley

Salt

Pepper

3 egg yolks

4 egg whites

Fresh Tomato Sauce (see Eggplant Baked with Three Cheeses for recipe)

Cook the livers and onion in the butter in a saucepan over medium heat. When livers are browned but still slightly pink in the center, stir in flour and cook another minute. Pour in Cognac and add seasonings. Transfer mixture to a blender or food processor. With machine running, drop in the egg yolks one by one. Turn machine off, scrape down the sides, and process again for a few seconds.

Preheat oven to 350°F. Whip egg whites until stiff peaks form. Fold the liver mixture into them. Pour into a generously buttered 2-quart (2000-ml) soufflé mold. Bake in a preheated 350°F. oven for 30 to 40 minutes, or until a knife plunged into the center comes out clean. Serve at once. Pass a bowl of Fresh Tomato Sauce separately.

BROWN RICE PILAU

Pilaw, pilaf, plov, pilav, or pilau, depending on which country you're in —Poland, France, Russia, Turkey—is rice cooked in butter or oil and baked with meat, fish, chicken, or vegetables added. This version makes a good side dish to serve with fish or meat, or serve it as a main course: start the meal with Chilled Avocado Soup with Buttermilk and then serve the pilau, accompanied by Tomatoes Baked with Goat Cheese, and Green Bean Salad with Pesto.

Serves 4 to 6

1 cup (250 ml) uncooked brown rice	2 medium tomatoes
3 tablespoons (45 ml) olive oil	2 teaspoons (10 ml) fresh thyme, or 1 teaspoon (5 ml) dried
1 small eggplant, about 1 pound (450 g)	½ teaspoon (3 ml) dried red pepper flakes
2 medium zucchini, about ¾ pound (337 g) total	Salt
1 large onion	2½ cups (625 ml) boiling water
1 red bell pepper	2 tablespoons (30 ml) minced parsley
1 medium clove garlic	

Cook the rice in oil in a heavy skillet over medium-high heat for about 5 minutes, stirring occasionally.

Cut eggplant and zucchini in 1-inch (25-mm) cubes. Slice onion in very thin rounds and cut pepper in thin strips. Chop the garlic. Add all of this to the skillet with the rice and cook over medium-high heat for about 5 minutes, until the vegetables begin to soften. Chop the tomatoes coarsely and add them. Stir in thyme, red pepper flakes, and salt. Transfer mixture to an oiled baking dish and pour in the boiling water. Cover the dish and bake pilau at 350°F. for about 75 minutes, or until rice and vegetables are tender. Sprinkle with minced parsley before serving.

BLACK BEANS AND RICE WITH ORANGES AND ONION SAUCE

In Latin America, beans know no social barriers—they are eaten by rich and poor alike. It is not necessary to soak beans; they do best just simmered over low heat (the amount of time varies considerably, depending on, among other things, the age and type of bean). Don't add salt or any kind of fat before the beans get tender or they're apt to stay tough. And, for heaven's sake, don't add baking soda to them. I forget what the purpose of that is supposed to be, but whatever it is it's a terrible idea because it will destroy the great nutritive value of the beans.

This makes a fine meal on its own, with Papaya, Onion, and Apple Salad. Or serve it at a buffet table to accompany ham or roast pork.

Serves 8 to 10

BEANS:

- 2 cups (500 ml) dried black beans
- 1 medium onion, minced
- 2 cloves garlic, minced
- 2 teaspoons (10 ml) fresh marjoram or thyme, or 1 teaspoon (5 ml) dried
- 1 bay leaf
- 8 cups (200 ml) water
- 1 cup (250 ml) white wine
- Salt
- Pepper

RICE:

- 2 cups (500 ml) long-grain rice
- 2 tablespoons (30 ml) olive oil
- 1 medium onion, minced
- 2 medium cloves garlic, minced
- 3 medium tomatoes, chopped
- 1 teaspoon (5 ml) dried oregano
- Salt
- Pepper
- 5 cups (1250 ml) boiling water

116

ONION SAUCE:

½ cup (125 ml) olive oil
⅓ cup (85 ml) lemon juice
2 teaspoons (10 ml) fresh oregano, or 1 teaspoon (5 ml) dried
2 tablespoons (30 ml) minced parsley

⅓ cup (85 ml) finely minced onion
1 medium clove garlic, minced
¼ teaspoon (1.5 ml) dried red pepper flakes

ORANGES:

3 to 4 large oranges

1 bunch watercress

OPTIONAL GARNISH:

Sour cream
Guacamole (see Cold
Carrot Soup with
Guacamole, or Crab Cakes
with Guacamole and
Cilantro-Lime Butter for
recipe)

Rinse the beans in a colander or strainer, picking through them to remove any pebbles or dirt. Place them in a kettle with the onion, garlic, marjoram or thyme, and bay leaf. Add 8 cups (2000 ml) water and simmer, partly covered, until beans are just tender. Add wine, salt, and pepper and continue simmering, uncovered, until beans are very tender and all liquid is absorbed.

To prepare the rice, rinse it in a strainer. Warm the olive oil in a skillet, then add rice, onion, and garlic. Stir over medium-high heat until onion is translucent. Stir in chopped tomatoes, oregano, salt, and pepper. Pour in boiling water, cover pan tightly, and simmer about 18 minutes, or until rice is tender and all liquid is absorbed.

To make the onion sauce, combine all ingredients in a bowl.

To prepare the oranges, peel them and cut into thin slices. Arrange them on a platter surrounded by watercress.

To serve, ladle beans over each portion of rice. Pass onion sauce and oranges separately, along with sour cream and/or Guacamole if desired.

ADVANCE PREPARATION: The beans may be made a day or two in advance. The onion sauce could be made up to a day in advance.

The rice could be made a few hours in advance and reheated carefully. The oranges may be sliced up to an hour in advance.

LASAGNE WITH CHICKEN AND MARSALA

Well-made lasagne with tomato sauce and lasagne verdi are both among the world's great dishes as far as I'm concerned. This elegant variation, fragrant with cheese and wine, proves how versatile lasagne can be. For a dazzling buffet supper, serve a large platter of Mâche with Warm Shiitake Mushrooms along with the lasagne, and Rhubarb Bavarois with Strawberry Sauce for dessert.

Serves 6 to 8

4 boneless chicken breasts, about 1 pound (450 g) each

POACHING LIQUID:

4 cups (1000 ml) chicken broth
1 bay leaf
⅛ teaspoon (.5 ml) dried red pepper flakes

3 sprigs fresh thyme, or 1 teaspoon (5 ml) dried
1 small whole clove garlic, peeled

LASAGNE:

6 tablespoons (90 ml) sweet butter
2 medium onions, minced
2 medium cloves garlic, minced
1 tablespoon (15 ml) flour
15 ounces (422 g) ricotta cheese
½ cup (225 ml) Marsala wine

1 pound (450 g) cooked lasagne noodles, preferably green
½ pound (225 g) Fontina cheese, grated
1 cup (250 ml) whipping cream
½ cup (125 ml) grated Parmesan

Place chicken breasts in a large saucepan or Dutch oven with the poaching ingredients. Bring to a boil and simmer, covered, about 15 minutes, or until chicken is tender. Remove chicken, reserving cook-

118

ing stock. When it is cool enough to handle, cut the chicken in bite-sized pieces.

In a large skillet, melt 4 tablespoons (60 ml) of the butter and add the onions. Cook over low heat until onions are translucent. Add garlic and cook another 30 seconds. Stir in flour, then add reserved cooking stock. Simmer mixture over very low heat, about 10 minutes, stirring occasionally. Stir in the ricotta, chicken, and Marsala.

To assemble the lasagne, arrange about a third of the cooked pasta in the bottom of a buttered lasagne pan or large baking dish. Pour in all the chicken mixture and top with another third of the pasta. Cover this with all the Fontina cheese, and end with the remaining pasta. Pour the cream over the top, sprinkle with Parmesan, and dot with remaining 2 tablespoons (30 ml) butter. Bake at 350°F. about 40 minutes, or until lasagne is hot and bubbly throughout and lightly browned on top.

VEGETABLES

*Then a sentimental passion of a vegetable fashion
must excite your languid spleen,
An attachment à la Plato for a bashful young potato, or
a not too French French bean!*

Gilbert and Sullivan

In the days before farming, when society still lived by hunting, fishing, and gathering, root vegetables (including various tubers and bulbs) probably saved the human race from extinction. Turnips, onions, and radishes might be dug from the ground when other sources of food could not be found. Furthermore, many of the root vegetables could be saved through the long winter months, whereas other gleaned vegetables, such as mushrooms, tender nettles, ferns, and other green things, were available only during mild weather.

Once our roaming ancestors began to settle down and domesticate wild plants, their vegetable repertoire expanded. Five thousand years ago, for example, Peruvian farmers raised the ancestor of what would eventually be known as the Irish potato, and they were among the first to cultivate beans.

Europeans were growing leafy plants such as cabbage and spinach by the first millennium A.D. But in most of Europe, and many other parts of the world, for that matter, vegetables never really became popular until the late eighteenth century. The upper classes preferred meals centered around meat and game; for the poor, vegetables merely added occasional spice to an otherwise bland diet based on legumes and grains. South American natives flavored their corn and beans with slivers of tomato and hot or mild peppers. In ancient Egypt, onions and leeks sometimes perked up the standard peasant diet of bread and beer. Root vegetables and occasional greens such as cabbage remained the staple vegetables in Europe at least through the medieval period.

Gradually, however, distinctive vegetable dishes began to evolve from peasant kitchens. As trade and exploration (and war) brought new ingredients and customs to different regions, and as kitchens became slightly less primitive and food somewhat less scarce, housewives came up with alternatives to such standard fare as cabbage boiled to smithereens with a chunk of fatback. People living close to the land —the ones who had access to the freshest, youngest, most flavorful vegetables—developed the sort of vegetable preparations that were the glory of peasant cooking. From southern France and Italy came tomato-based stews such as ratatouille and caponata. China produced stir-fried vegetables, Middle Eastern countries worked wonders with eggplant, and in Eastern Europe stuffed cabbage became an art form.

Contemporary technology has brought us some horrendous "improved" vegetables, such as tasteless tomatoes. But on the whole, the vegetables we eat on a year-round basis are fresher and more varied than has ever before been possible. Until a few years ago, how many Americans had heard of radicchio, spaghetti squash, or jícama? Who but home gardeners had access to finger eggplant, parsley root, or even red bell peppers? There are still many places in the United States suffering through the vegetable Dark Ages, but more and more of us can agree with Jean-Louis Palladin, of the restaurant Jean-Louis at Watergate, when he says, "The world is my market."

Spinach with Garlic and Pine Nuts in
Radicchio Cups

Fondant of Swiss Chard with Cream

Carrot Tart with Spinach "Crust"

Carrots with Honey and Fresh Mint

Broccoli with Wasabi

Cauliflower Sauté with Anchovies

Asparagus with Crème Fraîche and Chives

Lima Bean Purée with Rosemary and Buttermilk

Braised Leeks with Caper Cream Sauce

Julienned Parsnips and Snow Peas

Scalloped Onions

Glazed Onions

Parsley Root Purée

Sesame Spinach

Eggplant Baked with Three Cheeses

Potatoes with Garlic and Lemon Peel

Potato-Mushroom Gratin

Mushrooms Stuffed with Spinach and Pernod

Baked Tomatoes Stuffed with Kasha

Fresh Tomato Tart

Turnip Strudel

Tomatoes Baked with Goat Cheese

Baked Yams with Sour Cream and Chutney

Warm Grilled Vegetables

See also:

Zucchini Tian with Goat Cheese
Wild Mushroom Ragout
Tortellini in Brodo with Swiss Chard and Red Pepper

SPINACH with GARLIC and PINE NUTS in RADICCHIO CUPS

Several peasant dishes use a salad leaf as an edible food-container—Vietnamese cha gio *comes immediately to mind, where raw lettuce leaves are wrapped around a pork and shellfish filling.*

Serve this colorful and flavorful vegetable dish to accompany meats or poultry, or even seafood—it's good with Salmon with Soy Sauce and Lime, for instance.

Serves 4

2 bunches fresh spinach, about 2 pounds (900 g) total
1 tablespoon (15 ml) oil
2 medium cloves garlic, minced

2 tablespoons (30 ml) pine nuts
4 large whole radicchio leaves

Rinse spinach and place it in a large kettle. Cover and cook 2 or 3 minutes, or until spinach has just wilted (do not overcook). Transfer to a colander.

Add oil to kettle and cook garlic and pine nuts in it for about 1 minute, without letting garlic color. Squeeze excess water from spinach, add to garlic mixture, and toss over heat just long enough to reheat spinach.

Separate four large whole radicchio leaves from the head. Fill them with the spinach mixture.

FONDANT of SWISS CHARD with CREAM

Swiss chard is the most versatile of greens. Italian peasants use its leaves for stuffing pasta, poultry, and fish. In Provence the white stems are chopped and sautéed in olive oil and garlic. Swiss chard may be substituted in any recipe calling for spinach.

Fondant *means something like "melts-in-the-mouth," and that's what this dish should be: creamy and meltingly smooth. Try it with Duck with Black Pepper and Kumquats for a colorful Christmas dinner.*

Serves 4

1 bunch Swiss chard, about
1½ to 2 pounds (675 to
900 g)
½ cup chicken stock
⅓ cup (85 ml) whipping
cream or Crème Fraîche
(see Cornmeal Crêpes with
Crème Fraîche and Caviar
for recipe)

Salt
Pepper

With a sharp knife, cut Swiss chard into shreds. Place in a large saucepan or kettle with chicken stock and cream or Crème Fraîche and simmer, covered, for 10 minutes. With a slotted spoon, transfer chard to a serving bowl and keep it warm. Turn up heat and cook liquid remaining in saucepan rapidly for about 5 minutes, or until reduced by about half. Season with salt and pepper and pour over chard.

CARROT TART with SPINACH "CRUST"

Choose young, tender carrots rather than the big, strong-flavored ones we used to call "horse carrots." This very handsome orange and green tart may be served with most meat or poultry dishes. Or try it with a fish dish, such as Fish Fillets with Macadamia Nuts and Guinness.

Serves 6 to 8

1½ **pounds (675 g) carrots**	**Salt**
4 **tablespoons (60 ml) sweet**	1 **egg**
butter	½ **cup (125 ml) milk**
1 **tablespoon (15 ml)**	1 **bunch spinach, about 1**
ground cumin	**pound (450 g)**

Peel and grate carrots. Melt butter in a heavy skillet. Add carrots and cook over medium-low heat, stirring frequently, for about 3 minutes, or until carrots are just beginning to get tender. Stir in cumin and salt and allow carrots to cool slightly. Beat egg with milk and stir into carrot mixture.

Rinse spinach leaves and discard large stems. Shake off excess water and place spinach in a large kettle. Simmer, covered, about 30 seconds, or until leaves just begin to wilt. Uncover kettle immediately and remove from heat.

Generously butter a 9- to 10-inch (225- to 250-mm) ceramic or Pyrex quiche dish or pie pan. As soon as spinach is cool enough to handle, open leaves up one by one and arrange about half of them in a solid layer over bottom and sides of the pie pan. Pour in carrots and cover with remaining spinach leaves. Cover dish with foil.

Bake, covered, at 400°F. about 20 to 30 minutes, or until hot and steamy. To serve, cut in wedges.

ADVANCE PREPARATION: Tart may be assembled and re-frigerated for several hours, or overnight, before baking.

CARROTS with HONEY and FRESH MINT

People have been cultivating mint since at least the time of the ancient Egyptians and carrying slips of it with them whenever they move. Mint grows in a flash, hybridizes readily, is wildly fertile, and clones like mad. The result of this frenetic behavior is that there are extraordinary numbers of different kinds of mint; botanists can sometimes identify varieties only under a micro-scope. Cooks don't need to be so particular: use spearmint, peppermint, pineapple mint, or any other fresh mint from the herb garden or produce counter. For that matter, use dried mint if you have to.

This dish goes well with meat and poultry. Serve it with Chicken Breasts with Braised Shallots, Prosciutto, and Raspberry Vinegar, for example.

Serves 6

2 pounds (900 g) carrots
1 tablespoon (15 ml) butter
½ cup (125 ml) water
1 tablespoon (15 ml) honey
1 tablespoon (15 ml) soy
sauce

2 tablespoons (30 ml)
minced fresh mint, or 2
teaspoons (10 ml) dried

Peel carrots and slice thinly. Place them in a saucepan with butter, water, honey, and soy sauce. Simmer, covered, over very low heat for 20 to 30 minutes, or until carrots are tender but not mushy. Just before serving, stir in mint and reheat if necessary.

BROCCOLI with WASABI

Wasabi is the root of Japanese horseradish, commonly used in Japan to flavor sushi, sashimi, and other foods. It is dried, ground to a powder, and generally mixed with water to form a paste. Wasabi is greenish, fiercely hot, and guaranteed to enliven the taste of whatever it is served with. You can buy wasabi powder in stores that sell Japanese food products.

This dish can be served just about any time a green vegetable is called for.

Serves 4 to 6

1 teaspoon (5 ml) powdered
wasabi
1 teaspoon (5 ml) water
1 tablespoon (15 ml) soy
sauce

1 tablespoon (15 ml) sherry
or dry white wine
1 bunch broccoli, about 1½
pounds (675 g)
2 tablespoons (30 ml) oil

Dissolve wasabi in water and let sit, covered, for 10 minutes. Stir in soy sauce and sherry or white wine.

Cut broccoli into bite-sized pieces, peeling tough stems. Heat the oil in a wok or heavy skillet and add broccoli. Cook quickly, stirring constantly, for 3 to 5 minutes, or until broccoli is just tender but still crunchy. Turn off heat and stir in wasabi mixture. Serve immediately.

CAULIFLOWER SAUTÉ WITH ANCHOVIES

One of the oldest recipes in Western culinary history is the one for garum, an ancient Roman sauce based on preserved anchovies. Many peasant cultures that seem to have little else in common share a fondness for the salty/fishy bite of anchovies—for example, one of the best-known Vietnamese ingredients, nuoc nam, is based on anchovies, as is England's beloved Worcestershire sauce. Perhaps anchovies are exceptionally good at bringing out other flavors. In any event, they combine well with cauliflower, and the result is very compatible with many meat and chicken dishes. Try it with Lamb Tarts, for example.

Serves 4 to 6

1 head cauliflower, about 1
½ pounds (675 g)
1 tablespoon (15 ml) olive
oil
6 canned anchovies, chopped
4 medium cloves garlic,
minced

¼ teaspoon (1.5 ml) red
pepper flakes
1 tablespoon (15 ml) fresh
lemon juice
2 tablespoons (30 ml)
minced parsley

Trim and rinse cauliflower and break it into bite-sized florets. Steam or simmer in water to barely cover for about 8 minutes, or until cauliflower is just tender but still firm.

Heat olive oil in a heavy skillet. Add cauliflower, anchovies, garlic, and pepper flakes. Cook over medium heat, stirring frequently, until cauliflower is lightly browned. Stir in lemon juice and sprinkle with parsley.

ASPARAGUS WITH CRÈME FRAÎCHE AND CHIVES

The Greeks gathered wild asparagus. By 200 B.C. Roman peasants were cultivating it and even drying it to liven up soups and stews out of season. But it wasn't just the fine grassy flavor of asparagus that was appreciated by classical gourmands—they were convinced that the vegetable was a powerful aphrodisiac.

Buttered asparagus is an old favorite, but the rich sharpness of Crème

Fraîche enhances the vegetable even further. It can be served this way either as a first course or almost any time a green vegetable is called for.

Serves 4

1 **pound (450 g) asparagus**
1 **cup (250 ml) Créme Fraîche (see Cornmeal Crêpes with Crème Fraîche and Caviar for recipe)**

1 **tablespoon (15 ml) minced fresh chives**

Rinse asparagus and snap off the stem ends. Steam or simmer it in water until tender but not mushy, about 10 to 15 minutes, depending on size of stalks. Arrange on a serving platter. Top with Crème Fraîche and sprinkle with chives.

LIMA BEAN PURÉE WITH ROSEMARY AND BUTTERMILK

Short, fat, dried greenish beans form the basis of many peasant meals. In France flageolets are popular, in Brazil a type of lima bean is part of the staple diet, and in the United States succotash, a traditional dish dating back to Native American cooking, is based on lima beans. Conveniently, the lima bean is one of the few vegetables that are almost as good frozen as fresh.

The texture of puréed lima beans is reminiscent of mashed potatoes. In fact, this dish could be served just about anytime you might otherwise serve mashed potatoes.

Serves 4 to 6

4 **cups fresh Fordhook lima beans, or 2 10-ounce (280-g) packages frozen**
1 **medium clove garlic, chopped**

2 **tablespoons (30 ml) olive oil**
½ **teaspoon (3 ml) dried rosemary**
1 **cup (250 ml) buttermilk**

If using frozen lima beans, defrost enough so that the block can be broken apart. Cook beans, along with the garlic, in olive oil over medium heat about 5 minutes, or until they just begin to color. Stir in rosemary and buttermilk. Simmer, covered, over very low heat for about 15 minutes, or until beans are very tender. Transfer mixture to a food processor and purée.

ADVANCE PREPARATION: Lima bean purée could be prepared up to a day ahead of time and heated in a covered baking dish in a 350°F. oven, or in a double boiler on top of the stove, before serving.

BRAISED LEEKS WITH
CAPER CREAM SAUCE

For some reason leeks have never been as popular in the United States as they are in Europe, where they are generally considered the most flavorful representative of the onion family. Leeks form the basis of many peasant dishes, such as Scottish cock-a-leekie and French poireaux gratinés. Leeks, by the way, are the national vegetable of Wales. Serve this with Chicken Shepherd's Pie or Lamb Tarts.

Serves 4 to 6

1 bunch leeks (about 3 medium leeks)	½ cup (125 ml) white wine
½ cup (125 ml) beef or veal stock	⅓ cup (85 ml) whipping cream
	1 teaspoon (5 ml) capers

Cut off roots and top 2 or 3 inches (50 to 75 mm) of the leeks. Cut each leek in half lengthwise and rinse thoroughly to flush out all dirt and grit. Cut in half crosswise and arrange leeks in a skillet. Pour in stock and wine, bring to a boil, and simmer, covered, for about 20 minutes, or until leeks are tender. With a slotted spatula, remove leeks to a dish.

Turn heat up to high under the cooking liquid. Add cream and boil, uncovered, about 5 minutes, or until reduced by about half. Stir in capers. Return leeks to pan and reheat if necessary.

JULIENNED PARSNIPS AND
SNOW PEAS

Until the potato arrived in Europe via Sir Walter Raleigh, parsnips were the vegetable everybody ate, especially peasants. When Colonial Americans settled in the New World they were true to their roots, so to speak, using parsnips in everything from soup to wedding cakes. Early American epicures even favored parsnip wine.

Our ancestors' enthusiasm for parsnips was not unwarranted, for this sturdy root vegetable has many virtues. In addition to pleasant flavor and low price, 8 ounces (225 g) of cooked parsnips contain a mere 76 calories along with a reasonable amount of vitamins A and C, potassium, and other essential minerals.

Serves 4 to 6

¼ pound (112 g) snow peas
3 parsnips, about ½ pound
(225 g) total
1 teaspoon (5 ml) oil

1 medium clove garlic,
minced
2 teaspoons (10 ml) soy
sauce

Slice the snow peas into two or three strips lengthwise. Peel the parsnips and cut into strips about the size of matches. Heat the oil in a wok or large skillet and add the vegetables. Cook over medium–high heat, tossing the vegetables so that they cook evenly, for about 2 minutes. Add the garlic and continue cooking another few minutes, until parsnips are just tender but not mushy. Stir in the soy sauce and cook another few seconds.

SCALLOPED ONIONS

"Scalloped" refers to something that has been baked in a sauce covered with bread crumbs and/or cheese. We usually associate potatoes with this rustic preparation, but onions fare equally well scalloped. Properly prepared, this is a fine way to serve vegetables, but in my junior high school Home Economics class we had to make something called "Scalloped Cabbage" that was essentially overcooked cabbage covered with hot Elmer's glue. How we loathed it!

These onions go very well with just about any meat or poultry. Try them with Lamb Tarts, Rabbit in White Wine with Fresh Sage, or Whole Wrapped Fish.

Serves 4 to 6

4 large white or yellow
onions
2 tablespoons (30 ml) sweet
butter

½ cup (125 ml) bread crumbs
½ cup (125 ml) grated
Parmesan
1 cup (250 ml) milk

Slice onions thinly. Grease a baking dish with about half the butter. Spread half the onions in the bottom of the dish. Top with half the bread crumbs and half the cheese. Top with the remaining onions, then pour in the milk. Sprinkle remaining bread crumbs and cheese over the top and dot with remaining butter.

Bake in a 375°F. oven for 35 to 40 minutes, until top is very brown.

ADVANCE PREPARATION: The dish may be assembled several hours or a day ahead of time and baked just before serving.

GLAZED ONIONS

It's no wonder that onions are the most widely used vegetable in the world: they are easy to grow, inexpensive, and can be stored throughout the winter. They are extremely flavorful and nutritious. It's a shame to use them mainly as a flavoring agent when they are delicious on their own. Serve this dish to accompany meats and poultry. Try it with Lamb Tarts, Carbonnade in Brioches with Tenderloin of Beef, or Chicken with Fresh Figs, Port, and Basil.

Serves 4 to 6

10 ounces (280 g) fresh pearl onions

1 tablespoon (15 ml) butter
¼ cup (60 ml) chicken stock

Drop the onions into a saucepan of boiling water and simmer about 7 minutes. Drain. When they are cool enough to handle, trim off the root ends and slip the skins off the onions.

Place the onions in a skillet with the butter and chicken stock. Cook over medium heat, stirring frequently, for 20 to 30 minutes, or until onions are brown and syrupy. Raise heat if necessary to promote browning.

PARSLEY ROOT PURÉE

Parsley root is a well-known winter vegetable in Europe, but few Americans are familiar with this long, white, carrotlike vegetable. Parsley root is finally beginning to show up in markets here, and home gardeners have started to appreciate its culinary possibilities. Cooked celery root is similar in flavor—use it if you can't find parsley root. The sharp flavor of parsley root pairs well with other robust foods. This purée goes particularly well with Lamb Tarts. Add Asparagus with Crème Fraîche and Chives and you'll have a memorable menu.

Serves 4 to 6

1 **bunch parsley root (5 to 6 roots)**	¼ **cup (60 ml) whipping cream**
1 **teaspoon (5 ml) lemon juice**	**Salt**
	Pepper

Rinse and scrape parsley roots. Slice and place in a saucepan with enough water to just cover. Stir in lemon juice and simmer, covered, about 8 minutes, or until tender. Drain and transfer parsley root to a food processor or blender. Add cream, salt and pepper and purée until smooth. Reheat if necessary.

SESAME SPINACH

It's hard to imagine European peasant cuisine without spinach. There would be no lasagne verdi *or other green pastas, no Greek* spanikopita *or spinach pie, no* tarte Niçoise *with spinach and pine nuts. But apparently Europe had to wait until the sixteenth century for spinach to be introduced by the Moors. This particular spinach preparation goes well with just about any meal.*

Serves 2 to 4

2 **cups (500 ml) cooked spinach leaves**	**Juice of ½ lemon**
2 **tablespoons (30 ml) olive oil**	2 **tablespoons (30 ml) grated Parmesan**
3 **tablespoons (45 ml) sesame seeds**	**Salt**
1 **medium clove garlic, minced**	**Pepper**

Drain spinach thoroughly, squeezing out excess water with your hands. Chop coarsely.

In a heavy skillet, heat the olive oil for a few seconds. Add the sesame seeds and cook them, stirring constantly, over medium heat until lightly browned. Stir in garlic and add spinach. Cook over low heat until spinach is warmed through. Squeeze the juice of ½ lemon over it, remove from heat, and sprinkle with Parmesan. Salt and pepper to taste.

EGGPLANT BAKED WITH THREE CHEESES

Living in a rural community with access to a variety of local cheeses is a wonderful gastronomic experience, but then so is living in an urban center where an enormous selection of cheeses from around the world is available. It is the latter state of bliss that this recipe addresses. Vary the cheese, experimenting with different types ranging from hard (cheddar, Jack, mozzarella, Fontina), to soft and mild (cream cheese, ricotta, creamy chèvres, etc.) to dry (Parmesan, Gruyère, tomme de Savoie).

Serves 4

1 **large eggplant, about 1½ pounds (675 g)**	½ **cup (125 ml) grated Fontina cheese**
2 **cups (500 ml) Fresh Tomato Sauce (recipe follows)**	½ **cup (125 ml) grated Parmesan**
½ **cup (125 ml) ricotta cheese**	**Salt**
	Pepper

Cut eggplant into slices about ½ inch (12 mm) thick and place them in a skillet or kettle with enough water to just cover. Simmer, covered, about 5 minutes, or until eggplant is tender but not mushy. Drain.

Place half the Fresh Tomato Sauce in the bottom of an oiled baking dish and arrange half the eggplant slices over it. Distribute all of the ricotta and half of the Fontina over the eggplant, then cover with the remaining eggplant. Top with the rest of the tomato sauce and Fontina and sprinkle with Parmesan. Salt and pepper to taste. Bake, uncovered, at 350°F. about 30 minutes, or until dish is bubbly and lightly browned on top.

FRESH TOMATO SAUCE

1 **medium onion, minced**	2 **tablespoons (30 ml) olive oil**
1 **medium clove garlic, minced**	**Salt**

Pepper
4 **tomatoes, peeled and chopped**
2 **tablespoons (30 ml) minced fresh basil, or 1 teaspoon (5 ml) dried**

2 **teaspoons (10 ml) fresh thyme, or 1 teaspoon (5 ml) dried**

Cook onion and garlic in oil until translucent but not brown. Add remaining ingredients and simmer, uncovered, about 15 minutes, or until excess juices have mostly cooked away.

POTATOES with GARLIC and LEMON PEEL

I once spent a few summer weeks in a hot little town called Draguignan, in the hills behind Saint-Tropez. Because of a complicated series of misadventures, I had arrived at the height of the tourist season on the Riviera, with two small children and no place to stay. All hotels and pensions and even the campgrounds in the region were filled, but just before my concern escalated to panic a perfect stranger, a prosperous farmer's wife, offered me the use of her family's brand new "villa." They had not yet made the move from the old farmhouse and were happy to have my children and me spread our sleeping bags out in the big, empty house. Among the other things that happened during the dreamlike weeks we spent there: my sons learned to swim in the public pool in Draguignan, and I learned to make potatoes flavored with garlic and lemon peel, Italian in feeling just like many of the local people, and called pommes de terre Draçenoises. *I find that many of these sturdy regional specialties marry well with the assertive flavors of today's cuisine. Try this with Leg of Lamb with Pesto, for example, or Salmon with Soy Sauce and Lime.*

Serves 6

2 **pounds (900 g) potatoes**
¼ **cup (60 ml) olive oil**
Salt
Pepper
⅛ **teaspoon (.5 ml) nutmeg**
1 **tablespoon (15 ml) grated lemon rind**

¼ **cup (60 ml) minced parsley**
2 to 3 **medium cloves garlic, finely minced**
2 **anchovies, sliced**
Juice of 1 lemon

Boil potatoes until tender, about 20 to 30 minutes, depending on size. Peel and slice them. In a heavy skillet, sauté the potatoes in oil, turning frequently, until golden brown. Season with salt, pepper, nutmeg, and lemon rind.

Mix parsley, garlic, and anchovies together. Stir in the lemon juice. Just before serving, toss the potatoes with this mixture.

POTATO-MUSHROOM GRATIN

Potatoes were a peasant staple in much of Northern Europe for several generations, and they were also popular in the United States until their reputation declined for a couple of decades in the mid twentieth century. Happily, they are once again viewed as a highly nutritious food that is not fattening unless smothered in sour cream or fried in oil.

Serve this with Veal Paprikás, or Chicken Breasts with Braised Shallots, Prosciutto, and Raspberry Vinegar.

Serves 4 to 6

1 pound (450 g) baking potatoes	1 pound (450 g) mushrooms, sliced
1 cup (250 ml) milk	1 medium onion, minced
⅛ teaspoon (.5 ml) nutmeg	1 tablespoon (15 ml) oil
Salt	½ cup (125 ml) bread crumbs
Pepper	
6 tablespoons (90 ml) sweet butter	

Boil potatoes until tender. Peel and mash them, beating in the milk, nutmeg, salt, pepper, and 3 tablespoons (45 ml) of the butter. Reserve.

In a skillet, cook mushrooms and onion in 1 tablespoon (15 ml) of the butter and 1 tablespoon (15 ml) oil until mushrooms are soft and onions translucent.

Generously butter a 2-quart (2000-ml) baking dish. Sprinkle with half the bread crumbs. Spread a third of the potatoes in the bottom and top with half the mushrooms. Add another third potatoes, remaining mushrooms, and remaining potatoes. Sprinkle remaining bread crumbs over top and dot with remaining butter. Bake at 350°F. about an hour, or until top is browned and crisp.

MUSHROOMS STUFFED with SPINACH and PERNOD

Adding a splash of anise-flavored Pernod to traditionally stuffed mushrooms makes them taste a little like oysters Rockefeller, if you can imagine such a thing without the oysters. They'll liven up traditional meals, too: surround a Christmas turkey with them, for example, or plain roast chicken or beef. Or serve them with Rice with Black-eyed Peas and Sun-dried Tomatoes for a fine meatless dinner.

Serves 6

6 large mushrooms
½ cup (125 ml) cooked spinach, finely chopped
1 medium clove garlic, minced
2 tablespoons (30 ml) bread crumbs
1 teaspoon minced fresh tarragon, or ½ teaspoon (3 ml) dried

2 tablespoons (30 ml) Pernod
2 green onions, thinly sliced
Salt
Cayenne

Carefully remove stems from mushrooms and mince stems, reserving the caps. Purée remaining ingredients in food processor or blender. Spoon mixture into mushroom caps. Place under broiler or in a 500°F. oven for 3 to 5 minutes, or until very hot.

ADVANCE PREPARATION: Mushrooms may be stuffed up to a day ahead of time if desired and broiled just before serving.

BAKED TOMATOES STUFFED with KASHA

Kasha, sometimes called bulgur, is a staple in Russia and Poland, where it is eaten in soups and stews, with eggs and meat and cabbage, and even sweetened for dessert. It makes a fine, nutritious stuffing for baked tomatoes. You can buy kasha in almost any market. Follow directions on the box for cooking it.

Serves 4

4 large tomatoes

1 cup (250 ml) cooked kasha

1 onion, minced

2 medium cloves garlic, minced

½ cup (125 ml) diced red bell pepper

2 tablespoons (30 ml) oil

¼ cup (60 ml) pine nuts

½ teaspoon (3 ml) dried sage

1 teaspoon (5 ml) dried thyme

1 tablespoon (15 ml) lemon juice

½ teaspoon (3 ml) dried red pepper flakes

Salt to taste

Cut the tops off tomatoes and carefully scrape out the flesh. Chop the flesh coarsely and mix it with the kasha.

Cook the onion, garlic, and bell pepper in oil over medium heat until soft. Stir in the kasha and all remaining ingredients. Pack the mixture into the tomato shells. Place them in a baking dish and cover the dish with foil. Bake at 350°F. 30 to 40 minutes, or until tomatoes are very soft and skins are starting to split.

FRESH TOMATO TART

This is a wonderful dish to accompany meats, poultry, or fish, or to enjoy on its own as a light dish on a summer day with a big green salad. Serve it with Roast Chicken with Garlic and Fresh Ginger, and Leaf Lettuce with Cayenned Walnuts.

Serves 4 to 6

1 Herbed Pie Crust (recipe follows)

4 to 6 large ripe tomatoes

1 cup (250 ml) flour

2 teaspoons (10 ml) curry powder

Salt

Pepper

½ cup (125 ml) sweet butter

Preheat oven to 375°F. Fit pie crust into a 10- to 12-inch (250- to 300-mm) quiche pan. Bake it at 375°F. for 15 minutes.

Slice tomatoes and dredge them in flour seasoned with curry powder, salt, and pepper. Melt butter in a heavy skillet and sauté the tomatoes in it until they are lightly browned, turning once. Arrange them in the partially baked pie crust and return to oven for about 20 minutes, or until crust is lightly browned.

HERBED PIE CRUST

1½ cups (375 ml) all-purpose flour	6 tablespoons (90 ml) butter
⅓ cup (85 ml) minced fresh herbs (parsley, chives, dill, basil, etc.)	2 tablespoons (30 ml) oil
	3 tablespoons (45 ml) water

Place flour and herbs in food processor. Cut butter in about six pieces and add it along with the oil. With five or six on-off motions, process mixture until crumbly. With the motor running, pour in the water all at once. As soon as the dough begins to stick together, turn machine off. Gather dough into a ball and refrigerate for 30 minutes if possible. Roll or press dough into pie pan.

TURNIP STRUDEL

The word turnip *usually conjures up visions of stodgy stews full of soggy vegetables. But turnips really do have a bright flavor and pleasant texture when they're treated right. I broke with tradition and served this strudel with Thanksgiving dinner last year, and even my children came back for seconds.*

Filo pastry leaves can be bought in most supermarkets. For a large group, double the recipe and fill two pans.

Serves 6 to 8

3 cups (750 ml) shredded raw turnips (about 4 medium turnips)	2 eggs
	2 medium cloves garlic, chopped
⅓ cup (85 ml) chicken broth	⅛ teaspoon (.5 ml) cayenne pepper
1 large onion, minced	Salt
2 tablespoons (30 ml) sweet butter	½ cup (125 ml) butter
½ pound (225 g) feta or other hard goat cheese	½ pound (225 g) filo pastry leaves

Place shredded turnips in a colander and let drain about 10 minutes. Squeeze out excess moisture with your hands. Transfer turnips to a kettle and add chicken broth. Simmer, uncovered, stirring frequently, about 5 minutes, or until tender but not mushy.

Cook onion in 2 tablespoons butter (30 ml) over low heat until translucent but not browned. Add to turnips.

In a blender or food processor, beat together feta, eggs, garlic, cayenne, and salt. Stir into the turnip mixture.

Melt the ½ cup (125 ml) butter. Brush bottom and sides of a 10 × 12-inch (250 × 300-mm) baking pan, or a lasagne pan, with some of the butter. Cut the filo leaves to the approximate size of the baking dish. Carefully peel off one leaf and place in bottom of pan. Brush with melted butter, then cover with another filo leaf. Repeat until about half the filo is used. Spread the turnip mixture over this and cover with remaining filo leaves, brushing melted butter over each one.

Preheat oven to 350°F. Bake strudel about 1 hour, or until well browned. Cut in squares to serve.

ADVANCE PREPARATION: Strudel may be assembled 1 or 2 days ahead of time and refrigerated until ready to bake, or kept in the freezer for up to 2 weeks.

TOMATOES BAKED WITH GOAT CHEESE

It's hard to think of any other fruit or vegetable that has as many uses in Western cooking as the tomato. Used in salads, soups, stews, and sauces, where would peasant cooking be without the tomato? And yet Europeans wouldn't touch tomatoes for about a hundred years after they were brought back from the New World. And in the United States tomatoes didn't really gain acceptance until the late nineteenth century!

Serve these flavorful tomatoes with Black-eyed Peas with Garlic and Parsley, or Deep-dish Drumstick Pie.

Serves 6

6 medium tomatoes	Salt
3 medium cloves garlic, minced	4 ounces (112 g) soft goat cheese (see Note)
1 teaspoon (5 ml) thyme	½ cup (125 ml) bread crumbs
⅛ teaspoon (.5 ml) cayenne	

NOTE: Try to get soft goat cheese in a log shape for easiest slicing.

There are several domestic brands in that shape, or buy a French import such as Montrachet or Bucheron.

Cut a slice off the top of each tomato at the stem end. With a spoon, scoop seeds and flesh into a bowl. Stir in garlic, thyme, cayenne, and salt. Fill tomatoes with this mixture. Arrange them on a baking sheet.

Cut cheese into six slices, placing one slice on the top of each tomato. Sprinkle bread crumbs over the top of each. Bake in a 375° F. oven about 30 to 35 minutes, or until tomatoes are soft and browned on top.

BAKED YAMS WITH SOUR CREAM AND CHUTNEY

A New World tuber, the sweet potato (Ipomoea batatas) *isn't actually a potato at all. A yam isn't a potato, either, and it isn't even a sweet potato —it's another tuber altogether, whose scientific name is* Dioscorea bulbifera. *Botany isn't always easy, but this recipe is. Try it with Game Hens or Quail with Mole Sauce, or with a simple beef roast or roast chicken.*

Serves 6

6 yams or sweet potatoes
2 cups (500 ml) sour cream
2 cups (250 ml) mango
   chutney or other fruit
   chutney

Scrub yams and prick them with a fork. Bake at 375°F. about 45 to 50 minutes, or until soft.

In a bowl, stir together sour cream and chutney. When yams are done, cut them in half and top each with a dollop of the sour cream mixture. Pass the rest of it in a bowl.

WARM GRILLED VEGETABLES

Tiny eggplants, young zucchini, and other vegetables almost as small and fresh as if they had just come from the garden are turning up in markets these days. When you can find them, try grilling or broiling. Serve them a little warmer than room temperature, as a first course or as an accompaniment to Carbonnade in Brioches with Tenderloin of Beef, Deep-dish Drumstick Pie, or Salmon with Soy Sauce and Lime.

Serves 4

3 or 4 small eggplants, or 1 medium, about ½ pound (225 g) total
2 small zucchini, about ½ pound (225 g) total
2 Belgian endives
1 red bell pepper
4 medium mushrooms

¼ cup (60 ml) olive oil
2 teaspoons (10 ml) lemon juice
Salt
2 teaspoons (10 ml) minced fresh parsley
Freshly ground black pepper

OPTIONAL GARNISH:
Black olives

If using small eggplants, trim them and cut in half lengthwise. If using one medium eggplant, cut in half lengthwise and cut each half into very thin slices lengthwise.

Cut zucchini in eighths lengthwise.

Cut each endive into quarters lengthwise.

Cut bell pepper into quarters lengthwise. Cut off stem and membrane. Place the quarters, skin side up, under a broiler and cook until skin is bubbly and blackened. When pepper is cool enough to handle, peel skin off. Cut each quarter in half.

Arrange all vegetables, including the whole mushrooms, in a single layer on one or two oiled baking sheets. Mix together olive oil, lemon juice, and salt, and brush mixture liberally over the vegetables. A few minutes before serving, place vegetables under a hot broiler (or over hot coals) for about 5 minutes, or until vegetables have softened and browned. Transfer carefully to a platter or to four serving plates. Sprinkle with parsley and freshly ground pepper; garnish with olives if desired. Keep vegetables warm until ready to serve.

ADVANCE PREPARATION: The vegetables will taste even better if you assemble them up to a few hours ahead of time, letting them marinate in the olive oil mixture. Keep them loosely covered so they don't dry out.

DESSERTS

"O, a wonderful pudding!"

Charles Dickens

In the beginning there was honey. There were also dates and figs and berries to satisfy the human longing for sweet tastes. But there was no sugar, except in tropical Asia. Sugar was first cultivated in Bengal, the Persians were the first to refine it, and the Spanish introduced it to the West Indies. But sugar did not become commonplace in Europe until the late eighteenth century.

There was no chocolate, except in South America; the Spanish conquistadors brought chocolate back to Europe with them in the sixteenth century. There was no maple syrup, except in North America. But in North America there was no honey, until honeybees were introduced by the Europeans in the mid 1600s.

In spite of these missing ingredients, every culture produced desserts of one kind or another. Honey cakes were served in ancient Greece and at Mesopotamian feasts, and the Chinese were writing about honey cakes as far back as the third century B.C. The Arab and Indian worlds were very keen on sweets—in fact, the Arabs introduced Europeans to confections such as nougat and marzipan. Every country had its own sort of custard, pudding, or flan. Various kinds of jellied desserts were popular in the Middle Ages. As pastry-making developed, different cultures created variations on the highest form of the art, tissue-thin layers of dough baked until flaky: the Austrians created strudel, the Balkan states produced baklava, and the French came up with cream-filled mille-feuilles, or napoleons.

But for the average peasant, elaborate desserts and baked goods were eaten only on special occasions such as weddings and holidays: Christmas pudding in the British Isles, French Epiphany cake *(gâteau des rois),* Russian Easter *paskha,* Dutch *speculaas* to celebrate St. Nicholas on December 25, and so on. Everyday desserts were very simple—a piece of fresh fruit or a fruit compote is the standard peasant dessert. Sometimes the fruit is baked or poached, or incorporated into various kinds of pies or puddings.

"Comfort me with apples," says the Song of Solomon, and indeed, although we would all be better off if we ate more apples and less chocolate mousse, the fact is that even the humblest dessert soothes, satisfies, comforts us.

Rhubarb Bavarois with Strawberry Sauce

Mango Fool

Poached Meringues in Strawberry Sauce

Chocolate Trifle with Raspberries

Fresh Orange Cake with Bitter Chocolate Sauce

Chocolate Pudding with Praline

Honey-Quince Tart

Pears Baked with Cassis

Pear Caramel Compote

Maple-Walnut Clafouti with Apples

Cranberry-Apple Streusel

Cranberry Christmas Pudding with Gingered Hard Sauce

Fresh Ginger Gingerbread

Upside-down Blueberry Tart

Chestnut Chocolate Crème

Walnut Bread Pudding with Apricot Rum Sauce

Macadamia-Mocha Cheesecake

RHUBARB BAVAROIS WITH STRAWBERRY SAUCE

A native of Asia, rhubarb first made its way into the gardens of Europeans peasants via the monasteries, where it was grown as a medicinal plant. By the mid-nineteenth century, stewed rhubarb and rhubarb pie were among America's most popular desserts.

A fresh fruit bavarois is a fine dessert indeed, and not really so very difficult to prepare. If there is a trick to it, it is simply to make sure that everything else is really cold before folding in the whipped cream. I learned this the hard way once, via a soupy mess that never did gel. (I dished it into bowls anyway, spooned whipped cream over the top, and called it "dessert fruit soup." Everyone lapped it up happily, proving once again that culinary disasters are frequently redeemable.)

Serves 6 to 8

RHUBARB:

1 pound (450 g) fresh rhubarb

½ cup (125 ml) sugar
1 tablespoon (15 ml) water

CUSTARD:

3 egg yolks
1 cup (250 ml) milk
¼ cup (60 ml) sugar

½ teaspoon (3 ml) vanilla
1 package (1 tablespoon [15 ml]) gelatin

145

⅓ cup (85 ml) hot water

½ cup (125 ml) whipping
cream

STRAWBERRY SAUCE:

1 pint (500 ml) fresh
strawberries, or 1 package
frozen

2 tablespoons (15 ml) sugar
(optional)

Rinse the rhubarb and slice it. Place in a saucepan with ½ cup (125 ml) sugar and 1 tablespoon (15 ml) water. Simmer, covered, over low heat for about 15 minutes, or until rhubarb is very soft. Chill.

Combine egg yolks, milk, and ¼ cup (60 ml) sugar in a double boiler. Cook over simmering water, stirring constantly, until custard is just thick enough to coat the back of the spoon. Stir in vanilla. Mix gelatin into ⅓ cup (85 ml) hot water, stirring to dissolve. Stir mixture into custard. Strain into a bowl and chill.

Whip cream until stiff peaks form. When rhubarb and custard are cool, mix them together. Gently fold whipped cream into mixture. Pour into a lightly oiled loaf pan or other mold and refrigerate several hours, or until firm.

To make strawberry sauce, purée berries in a food processor or blender. Add sugar to taste if you wish.

To serve, unmold the *bavarois* on a platter and surround with Strawberry Sauce.

MANGO FOOL

Britain's fresh fruit fools are true country desserts. Made from ripe fruit and freshly whipped cream, what better way can there be to wind up a grand meal than with this fresh-tasting, fruit-sweetened, pastel orange treat?

Serves 4 to 6

1 ripe mango

½ pint (250 ml) whipping
cream

OPTIONAL GARNISH:
Fresh raspberries

Peel the mango and cut flesh away from the large seed. Place fruit in food processor or blender and purée it. Whip cream stiffly and fold it into the puréed mango. Transfer to a bowl and chill. To serve, spoon onto individual dessert plates and surround with fresh raspberries if desired.

ADVANCE PREPARATION: May be made several hours ahead of time.

POACHED MERINGUES IN
STRAWBERRY SAUCE

All children, peasant or otherwise, growing up in France or England are treated to a homey dessert called floating island, or oeufs à la neige, *which features poached meringues bobbing around on top of a light custard. Using puréed fruit instead of custard makes a low-calorie, very refreshing, attractive, and easy-to-make dessert.*

Substitute raspberries of blueberries for the strawberries if you wish, or use a combination of both. Strawberries must be fresh, but frozen raspberries are fine.

Serves 6

2 **egg whites**
½ **cup (125 ml) sugar**
4 **cups (1000 ml) water**

2 **cups (500 ml) fresh strawberries**

Beat egg whites until soft peaks form. Sprinkle ¼ cup (60 ml) of the sugar over them and continue beating just until stiff.

Bring 4 cups (1000 ml) water to a boil in a skillet, then turn heat down to simmer. Scoop up a spoonful of meringue with a tablespoon; with another spoon, round off the top of the meringue so that it is fairly evenly shaped. Drop into simmering water, adding as many meringues as will fit without crowding. Poach for about a minute, then carefully turn over and cook the other side another minute or so. Remove with a slotted spoon and drain on a clean tea towel or dish towel (do not use a paper towel, which tends to shred and cling to the meringue). Repeat until all egg white is used.

Purée berries in blender or food processor along with the remaining sugar; if using raspberries, strain mixture through a sieve. Pour sauce into a serving bowl and float meringues on top. Chill thoroughly.

CHOCOLATE TRIFLE WITH RASPBERRIES

I like to serve this chocolate variation of an old British favorite for a large group, doubling the recipe if necessary. It's a great treat in the summer when fresh raspberries are in season, but I use frozen raspberries when I have to and it's still good.

Serves 6 to 8

CHOCOLATE SPONGE:
6 ounces (168 g) semisweet chocolate

⅓ cup (85 ml) sugar

6 eggs, separated

1 cup (250 ml) all-purpose flour

1 teaspoon (5 ml) vanilla

CUSTARD SAUCE:
4 egg yolks

½ cup (125 ml) sugar

2 cups (500 ml) milk

1 teaspoon (5 ml) vanilla

ASSEMBLING TRIFLE:
¾ (180 ml) cup sherry

2 pints (1000 ml) fresh raspberries, or 2 10-ounce (280-g) packages frozen

¾ cup (180 ml) whipping cream

Line an 11 × 16 × ½-inch (275 × 400 × 12-mm) baking sheet with waxed paper or foil. Butter it generously and set aside.

Preheat the oven to 375°F.

Break chocolate in pieces, place in top of double boiler, and melt over simmering water.

Place ⅓ cup (85 ml) sugar, 6 egg yolks, and flour in food processor or mixing bowl. Beat until pale and creamy. Beat in 1 teaspoon (5 ml) vanilla. While still beating, pour in chocolate.

In a separate bowl, beat 6 egg whites until stiff peaks form. Using a rubber spatula, fold chocolate mixture into them.

Spread mixture evenly over the prepared pan. Bake in a 375°F. oven about 15 minutes, or until mixture begins pulling away from edges of pan. Remove from oven and cover with a towel for about 10 minutes. Then carefully peel cake away from its backing.

To make the custard, place 4 egg yolks and ½ cup (125 ml) sugar in a heavy saucepan and whisk until light. Whisk in the milk and place pan over medium heat. Stir constantly until mixture begins to thicken, but do not boil. Remove from heat and stir in 1 teaspoon (5 ml) vanilla. Strain custard into a bowl and refrigerate.

To assemble the trifle, cut the cake into four pieces and sprinkle them with the sherry. Arrange them in a bowl alternating with raspberries. Pour custard in. Whip cream and spread it over the top. (Don't worry if the cake falls apart—just arrange the pieces in layers with the berries.)

ADVANCE PREPARATION: The cake and custard may be made up to a day ahead of time. The trifle may be assembled up to an hour before serving.

FRESH ORANGE CAKE WITH
BITTER CHOCOLATE SAUCE

If you can possibly find blood oranges, by all means use them in this recipe, in spite of what several noted food writers have to say about Spain's beautiful red oranges: "They frighten American women," writes John McPhee ("possibly the only thing that does," adds Waverly Root). "American women are put off by the color," James Trager assures us. I think the stiff price might put off a good many people, but if you've never tasted this sweet, ruby-red member of the citrus family, you're in for a pleasant surprise. And I doubt that anyone will be frightened.

Serves 4 to 8

FRESH ORANGE CAKE:

4 eggs, separated
½ cup (125 ml) sugar
2 tablespoons (30 ml) Grand Marnier or other orange-flavored liqueur

2 fresh oranges, preferably blood oranges
1¼ cups (310 ml) unbleached flour

BITTER CHOCOLATE SAUCE:

6 ounces (168 g) [6 squares] bitter chocolate 2 tablespoons (30 ml) sugar	1 cup (250 ml) water 1 cup (250 ml) milk

Preheat the oven to 350°F. Generously butter a 9-inch (225-mm) round cake pan.

Beat the egg yolks and ½ cup (125 ml) sugar together until they are thick and light-colored and form a ribbon. Beat in the orange liqueur. Grate the rind of both oranges, reserving the flesh. Add rind to the egg yolk mixture. Fold in the flour.

Beat the egg whites until stiff peaks form. Delicately fold into the egg yolk mixture. Pour into the buttered cake pan and bake in a preheated 350°F. oven about 30 minutes, or until cake is lightly colored and has just begun to shrink from sides of pan. Remove from oven and let sit for about 5 minutes, then turn out on a rack to cool.

To make the sauce, place chocolate, 2 tablespoons (30 ml) sugar, and water in the top of a double boiler. Stir over simmering water until chocolate has melted. Whisk in milk and cook another 2 or 3 minutes, or until mixture just begins to simmer. Remove from heat and chill.

To serve, cut the oranges in thin slices. Cut cake in slices and arrange each slice on its side on an individual dessert plate. Arrange a layer of overlapping orange slices over the top of each piece of cake and pour a pool of chocolate sauce around it.

CHOCOLATE PUDDING with PRALINE

Every culture has its favorite custard or pudding. Hawaiians make it with coconuts, Colonial Americans used corn. France's crème caramel *is called* flan *in Spain. In England pudding is wrapped up and boiled. China's Eight Precious Treasure Rice Pudding, with candied and preserved fruits, ranks as one of the world's most lavish puddings, while America's favorite chocolate pudding is one of the simplest. Incidentally, it is an appropriate dessert for this continent because chocolate (from the Aztec word* xocolatl) *was a Latin American native unknown in Europe until the mid-seventeenth century.*

Like most chocolate desserts, this one is fairly rich and filling. It is best served after a light meal. It would be the perfect way to end a dinner of Poached Cod with Fresh Sage Butter and Carrot Tart with Spinach "Crust," for example.

Serves 6 to 8

CHOCOLATE PUDDING:

¼ cup (60 ml) cornstarch
1 cup (250 ml) milk
1 cup (250 ml) half-and-half
5 egg yolks

½ cup (125 ml) sugar
8 ounces (225 g) [8 squares]
   bittersweet chocolate

PRALINE:

½ cup (125 ml) almonds,
   with skins on

2 tablespoons (30 ml) water
½ cup (125 ml) sugar

In the top of a double boiler, whisk together cornstarch, milk, half-and-half, egg yolks, and sugar. Add chocolate and stir over simmering water until mixture thickens to the consistency of light custard. Strain pudding into a bowl and refrigerate, covered, until cold, several hours or overnight.

To make praline, break or use a knife to cut the almonds into large chunks and spread them in the bottom of a greased metal pie tin or on a baking sheet. In a heavy saucepan, heat water and sugar together until it caramelizes (turns a light brown). Swirl pan occasionally. Pour mixture over the almonds, using extreme caution—caramel is fiercely hot. Allow to cool until it is very hard and solid. Break into chunks and pulverize them in a food processor.

To serve, divide chocolate pudding among six or eight individual dessert bowls or glass goblets. Sprinkle praline over the top of each.

HONEY-QUINCE TART

Peasants in pre-Christian Europe cultivated quinces. The ancient Greeks thought highly enough of the fruit to call it "the golden apple." The French gave it the unmelodious name coing, *but they appreciate its sweet flavor. Colonial Americans were also fond of this fruit, which they brought with them from the Old World. Unfortunately, it has fallen into disfavor in America today, perhaps because it can't be eaten raw. Buy a couple of quinces if you find them in the markets in late fall—they look, indeed, like elongated golden apples—and see if you don't like their distinctive rich and fruity flavor baked in a tart.*

Serves 8

2 large quinces, peeled, cored, and cut in large dice

1 tablespoon (15 ml) lemon juice

½ cup (125 ml) honey

CRUST:

1 cup (250 ml) unbleached flour

6 tablespoons (90 ml) butter

2 tablespoons (30 ml) oil

Salt

About ¼ cup (60 ml) cold water

OPTIONAL GARNISH:

Whipped cream

Combine quinces, lemon juice, and honey in a saucepan. Simmer, covered, about 15 minutes, or until tender. Purée in food processor or blender.

To make the crust, mix together flour, butter, oil and salt until mixture is crumbly. Add just enough water for mixture to hold together. Roll dough out to fit a 9-inch pie pan or quiche pan, prick crust with a fork and weight it down with another pie pan or special pie-crust beans to keep it from forming bubbles, and bake in a pre-heated 375°F. oven about 25 minutes, or until very lightly browned.

Spread honey-quince mixture in partially baked crust and bake at 375°F. about 20 minutes, or until tart is just beginning to show signs of browning. Serve at room temperature, plain or with whipped cream.

PEARS BAKED with CASSIS

Peasants first began cultivating pears in Asia and Europe around four thousand years ago. There are thousands of different varieties today. Crème de cassis, which imparts a berrylike flavor to the pears and turns them pink, is a distillation made from black currants. It is best known as the ingredient mixed with white wine to make the popular aperitif Kir.

Serve these pears as is, or top them with vanilla ice cream or whipped cream. This is a refreshing dessert to serve after a big meal.

Serves 6 to 8

6 **firm pears, such as bosc or d'Anjou**
Juice of ½ lemon
2 **cups (500 ml) crème de cassis**

½ **pound (225 g) hazelnuts (with or without skins), coarsely chopped**

OPTIONAL GARNISH:
Whipped cream or vanilla ice cream

Cut pears in half lengthwise. Peel them and remove stems and cores, dropping halves into a bowl of water with juice from ½ lemon to prevent discoloring.

Remove pears from water and place in a baking dish large enough to hold them in a single layer. Pour in crème de cassis, cover dish with foil, and bake at 350°F. about 40 minutes, or until pears are very tender. Chill thoroughly.

Toast nuts in a toaster oven or under a broiler until they are lightly browned. Reserve.

To serve, scatter nuts over pears. Or place pears in individual dessert bowls, top with whipped cream or ice cream, and sprinkle with nuts.

PEAR CARAMEL COMPOTE

This is a simple fruit compote, with the pears cooked in butter long enough to reduce them to a rich purée. An old-fashioned heavy iron skillet is the best thing to cook them in. Select pears that are ripe but firm—d'Anjou or Bosc are good types to use.

Serve 4 to 6

5 **medium pears**
1 **tablespoon (15 ml) sweet butter**
3 **tablespoons (45 ml) sugar**

2 **tablespoons (30 ml) Pear William or other pear brandy**

OPTIONAL GARNISH:
Crème Fraîche (see
Cornmeal Crêpes with
Crème Fraîche and Caviar
for recipe), or heavy
cream

Core and quarter pears but do not peel them. Chop them coarsely. Melt butter in a heavy skillet or kettle. Add pears and simmer, covered, about 15 minutes, or until pears are soft. Stir in the sugar and simmer another 10 minutes, uncovered. Mash mixture with a fork or purée it in food processor or blender. Return it to skillet. Continue cooking over medium-low heat for about 10 more minutes, until mixture has thickened and colored a little. Stir frequently to prevent scorching. Stir in pear brandy and remove from heat. Transfer compote to a bowl and chill for several hours or overnight.

To serve, divide mixture among individual dessert bowls or glass goblets. Top with a spoonful of Crème Fraîche or pass a pitcher of heavy cream separately.

MAPLE-WALNUT
CLAFOUTI WITH APPLES

Clafouti is an old, rural French dessert whose consistency is somewhere between custard and a very thick crêpe. It is always fruit-filled, with prunes, cherries, blueberries, or apples, depending on the season. Maple syrup turns this clafouti *into a Franco-American dessert. Serve it warm or at room temperature, plain or with cream or ice cream.*

Serves 6

2 tablespoons (30 ml) sweet butter
4 cups (1000 ml) sliced, unpeeled apples (about 4 medium apples)
1 cup (250 ml) milk
½ cup (125 ml) unbleached flour

3 eggs
1⅓ cups (335 ml) pure maple syrup
1 cup (250 ml) shelled walnuts, broken into coarse pieces

<u>OPTIONAL GARNISH:</u>
  **Whipped cream flavored
  with maple syrup**

Preheat oven to 375°F. Put butter in an 8–cup (2000-ml) oval or rectangular baking dish and place in oven until butter melts. Add apple slices and toss until they are well coated with butter.

Beat milk, flour, eggs, and ⅓ cup (85 ml) of the maple syrup together until smooth (may be done in blender or food processor). Pour mixture over apples. Sprinkle walnuts over the top.

Bake *clafouti* in a 375°F. oven for about 45 minutes, or until it is browned and a knife plunged into the center comes out clean. Pour the remaining maple syrup over the *clafouti* as soon as it comes out of the oven.

Serve warm or cold, plain or garnished with whipped cream flavored with maple syrup.

CRANBERRY-APPLE STREUSEL

Although "streusel" comes from the German word that means strewn or sprinkled, the concept of a simple fruit dessert baked with a crumb topping is found in many different peasant cuisines, especially in the British Isles—brown Betty and blackberry crumb are good examples.

Serves 6

2 cups (½ pound [225 g]) fresh or frozen cranberries

2 cups (500 ml) sliced apples (about 2 apples), skins left on

⅔ cup (170 ml) uncooked oatmeal

½ cup (125 ml) sugar

½ teaspoon (3 ml) cinnamon

¼ teaspoon (1.5 ml) grated nutmeg

4 tablespoons (60 ml) sweet butter

<u>OPTIONAL GARNISH:</u>
  **Heavy cream, whipped
  cream, yogurt, or vanilla
  ice cream**

Combine cranberries and apples in a greased 6–cup baking dish. Place oatmeal, sugar, cinnamon, and nutmeg in food processor. Cut butter in four pieces and add it to the oatmeal mixture. Process ingredients a few seconds, until mixture is crumbly. Sprinkle over fruit.

Bake at 400°F. for 25 to 30 minutes, or until browned on top. Serve warm or cold, with heavy cream, whipped cream, yogurt, or vanilla ice cream if desired.

CRANBERRY CHRISTMAS PUDDING
WITH GINGERED HARD SAUCE

In the British Isles, Christmas would hardly be worth celebrating without a Christmas pudding. The one Mrs. Cratchit brought forth was, as Dickens described it, "like a speckled canon-ball, so hard and firm, blazing with ignited brandy. . . ."

Fresh cranberries lighten the cannonball effect a bit, and their tartness is a nice foil to the unrelieved sweetness of most puddings.

Serves 8 to 10

PUDDING:
2 cups (500 ml) fresh bread crumbs
1 cup (250 ml) flour
¼ teaspoon (1.5 ml) nutmeg
1 teaspoon (5 ml) cinnamon
1 teaspoon (5 ml) baking soda
2 cups (500 ml) brown sugar
1 cup (250 ml) currants
1 cup (250 ml) white raisins
½ cup (125 ml) mixed candied fruit
¼ cup (60 ml) pulverized almonds (with or without skins)

1½ cups (375 ml) fresh or frozen cranberries
1 cup (250 ml) shredded suet
4 eggs
½ cup (125 ml) light or dark rum
½ cup (125 ml) orange juice or cranberry juice
¼ cup (60 ml) dark corn syrup
Salt

FOR FLAMING:
2 tablespoons (30 ml) rum

GARNISH:

**Gingered Hard Sauce
(recipe follows) or plain
hard sauce**

Combine all pudding ingredients in a large bowl. Transfer mixture to a large (7- to 8-cup) [1750- to 2000-ml] pudding bowl or other heatproof bowl, or use two smaller bowls. Cover the top with two sheets waxed paper, and a layer of aluminum foil large enough to overlap the rim of the bowl by about two inches (50 mm). Secure the foil around the rim of the bowl by wrapping string around it; then wrap string under the bowl and back over the top, with enough left over after you've tied it to use as a handle.

Place bowl in a large saucepan or kettle (on a rack if possible) and pour in enough boiling water to come three-quarters of the way up the outside of the bowl. Cover the pan and simmer over very low heat for 3 hours. Check water level occasionally.

Store pudding in the refrigerator until ready to use. To serve, simmer pudding in a panful of water for 2 hours. Unmold onto a serving platter. Heat 2 tablespoons (30 ml) rum in a saucepan for a few seconds, until it is just warm to the touch (do not overheat or it will not ignite). Hold a match to the rum in the saucepan, and as soon as it flames, pour it over the pudding. Serve immediately. Pass plain or Gingered Hard Sauce separately.

ADVANCE PREPARATION: Christmas puddings are traditionally made at least 3 months ahead of time—by people much better organized than myself! I seldom get to mine until the week before Christmas, but they're always delicious anyway.

GINGERED HARD SAUCE

Hard sauce is the traditional accompaniment for Christmas puddings. It is also good on fruitcake. A grating of fresh ginger adds a refreshing note to the traditional recipe.

10 tablespoons (150 ml) sweet
   butter, softened
3 cups (750 ml) powdered
   (confectioner's) sugar

2 tablespoons (30 ml) rum
½ teaspoon (3 ml) vanilla
2 tablespoons (30 ml) grated
   gingerroot

Beat all ingredients together by hand or in a food processor until thoroughly blended. Refrigerate several hours before serving so that the sauce hardens.

ADVANCE PREPARATION: May be made up to a week in advance and refrigerated.

FRESH GINGER GINGERBREAD

An old American favorite that we got from the British, gingerbread is traditionally made with dried ginger. Fresh gingerroot adds an intriguing depth of flavor.

Serves 6

2 tablespoons (30 ml) grated gingerroot	2½ cups (625 ml) all-purpose flour
1 egg	1½ teaspoons (8 ml) baking powder
3 tablespoons (45 ml) butter	1 teaspoon (5 ml) cinnamon
1 cup (250 ml) brown sugar	
½ cup (125 ml) molasses or dark corn syrup	

OPTIONAL GARNISH:
Whipped cream,
unflavored yogurt, or
vanilla ice cream

Preheat oven to 350°F.

Beat together gingerroot, egg, butter, brown sugar, and molasses until light and fluffy. Fold in flour, baking powder, and cinnamon. Pour into a greased 9-inch (225-mm) square baking pan and bake at 350°F. about 40 minutes, or just until a toothpick inserted in the center comes out clean. Serve warm or cold, plain or with whipped cream, yogurt, or ice cream.

UPSIDE-DOWN BLUEBERRY TART

I tend to agree with the people who think blueberries are the one fruit better cooked than raw—except in Maine, where the local blueberries are tiny and juicy. But even there, this is a good dessert.

Serves 6

1 pint (500 ml) fresh
  blueberries
1 tablespoon (15 ml) flour
1 tablespoon (15 ml) butter
4 tablespoons (60 ml) sugar

½ teaspoon (3 ml) cinnamon
½ cup (125 ml) red wine
1 9-inch (225-mm) Pie Crust
  (recipe follows)

Preheat oven to 375°F.

Toss the blueberries and flour together. Butter a 9-inch (225-mm) pie pan with 1 tablespoon (15 ml) butter and spread the berries in it. Sprinkle sugar and cinnamon over them and pour in the wine. Drape the pie crust loosely over them and bake in a 375°F. oven about 30 minutes, or until crust is brown.

PIE CRUST

¾ cup (180 ml) flour
4 tablespoons (60 ml) butter
3 tablespoons (45 ml) oil

Salt
About ½ cup (125 ml)
water

Blend together flour, butter, oil, and salt until mixture resembles a coarse meal. Add enough water to hold dough together. Roll into a circle about 9 inches (225 mm) in diameter.

CHESTNUT CHOCOLATE CRÈME

I spent one glorious childhood summer in a small village in Corsica. There was an oak forest nearby that impressed me for two reasons. One was the startling contrast between the cool darkness of the forest and the brilliant white light everywhere else; the other was that wild boars were said to roam the forest consuming a steady diet of chestnuts. I never saw one, but the very thought of them lurking in the shadows munching on nuts was enough to lend a heady sense of danger to the woods. I know now that these wild pigs, with their built-in chestnut stuffing, made fine eating, but I never tasted one. In fact, the only chestnuts I remember from those days were in that ubiquitous French dessert Mont Blanc, puréed chestnuts topped with whipped cream, which was my idea of bliss. So is this crème with chocolate, which is sort of a grown-up Mont Blanc.

Canned chestnuts are fine in this dessert, and infinitely easier to use than fresh.

Serves 6

6 ounces (168 g) [4 squares]
semisweet dark chocolate
1 cup (250 ml) puréed
chestnuts (about 1 pound
[450 g])

1 cup (250 ml) milk
2 tablespoons (30 ml) rum
½ pint (250 ml) whipping
cream
1 teaspoon (5 ml) vanilla

In a double boiler, over simmering water, melt the chocolate. Beat
it with the chestnuts, milk, and rum. Chill thoroughly.

Whip the cream and add vanilla. Divide chocolate mixture among
six dessert bowls or goblets. Top each with whipped cream.

WALNUT BREAD PUDDING WITH
APRICOT RUM SAUCE

*Bread pudding was possibly the most common dessert in peasant
households in the days before industry learned how to make bread last forever.
Many contemporary restaurants make bread pudding with brioches. Use that
if it's available, otherwise use good quality homemade-type white bread.*

Serves 4 to 6

2 cups (500 ml) stale bread,
cut in cubes
1½ (375 ml) cups milk
2 egg yolks
½ cup (125 ml) sugar

1 teaspoon (5 ml) vanilla
1 cup (250 ml) walnut
pieces, coarsely chopped
2 egg whites

APRICOT RUM SAUCE:

1 cup (250 ml) dried
apricots
1⅔ cups (420 ml) water
⅓ cup (85 ml) sugar

⅓ cup (85 ml) rum
½ teaspoon (3 ml) lemon
juice

Place the bread cubes in a large bowl.

In a saucepan, whisk together milk, egg yolks, sugar, and vanilla.
Stir over medium-low heat until mixture just comes to the boil. Strain
this custard over the bread cubes. Fold in the walnuts.

Preheat oven to 375°F. Beat the egg whites until stiff peaks form.
Fold them into the bread mixture. Pour into a generously buttered

1-quart (1000-ml) soufflé mold and bake at 375°F. about 1 hour, or until pudding is golden brown and firm. Cool completely. May be served cold or at room temperature.

To prepare sauce, combine apricots, water, and sugar in a saucepan. Simmer, uncovered, about 12 minutes. Stir in rum and lemon juice. Puree mixture in blender or food processor. Chill thoroughly.

When serving pudding, pass Apricot Rum Sauce separately.

MACADAMIA-MOCHA CHEESECAKE

This is the sort of rich, voluptuous dessert that is usually described as "sinful." The original version of this recipe was created by a student of mine in one of my cooking classes in California whose daughter used to send her large bags of macadamia-nut shavings from a processing plant in Hawaii. It's a recipe that lends itself to variation: I sometimes add a cup of crushed chocolate-wafer crumbs to the crust mixture for example. I've substituted ricotta cheese for cream cheese for a lighter cake, and I once covered the entire cake with fresh raspberries. A friend of mine made it with chocolate chips folded into the cream-cheese mixture and reported that the chocoholics she served it to remained in a state of bliss for days afterwards.

Serves 10 to 15

CRUST:
1½ cups (375 ml) chopped macadamia nuts

½ cup (125 ml) melted sweet butter

FILLING:
1 cup (250 ml) sugar
3 eggs
1½ pounds (675 g) soft cream cheese
8 ounces (225 g) [8 squares] semisweet chocolate
1 teaspoon (5 ml) instant coffee

1 tablespoon (15 ml) hot water
1 teaspoon (5 ml) vanilla
3 cups (750 ml) sour cream
¾ cup (180 ml) chopped macadamia nuts
¼ cup (60 ml) melted butter

OPTIONAL GARNISH:
Whipped cream

To make the crust, mix 1½ cups (375 ml) macadamia nuts and ½ cup (125 ml) melted butter together. Press mixture firmly against the bottom and sides of a well-greased 9-inch (225-mm) springform pan. Chill at least 30 minutes.

For filling, beat 1 cup (250 ml) sugar and eggs together until light, then beat in cream cheese. Melt the chocolate and beat it into the mixture. Dissolve the coffee in 1 tablespoon (15 ml) hot water and add it along with the vanilla. Beat in the sour cream, then fold in the ¾ cup (180 ml) macadamia nuts and ¼ cup (60 ml) melted butter.

Preheat the oven to 350°F.

Pour the batter into the chilled pie shell. Bake at 350°F. for 45 minutes. Remove from oven even if the filling still seems very liquid —it will solidify with chilling.

Chill the cake thoroughly. To serve, remove the sides of the spring-form pan and decorate the top with whipped cream if desired.

ADVANCE PREPARATION: The cheesecake may be made up to a day in advance. Or make it up to a week in advance and freeze it.

SUGGESTED MENUS

FALL DINNER

Crab Chowder with Crème Fraîche and Lime

Wild Mushroom Ragout

Baked Polenta with Red Peppers

Spinach with Garlic and Pine Nuts in Radicchio Cups

Honey-Quince Tart

FIRESIDE SUPPER FOR TWO

Ham Steaks with Spinach and Madeira

Baked Yams with Sour Cream and Chutney

Cranberry-Apple Streusel

SUPER BOWL SUPPER

Walnut-Garlic Dip with Raw Vegetables

Chicken Shepherd's Pie

Tomatoes Baked with Goat Cheese

Fresh Ginger Gingerbread

HALLOWEEN BUFFET

Butternut Soup with Orange Crème Fraîche

Black Beans and Rice with Oranges and Onion Sauce

Papaya, Red Onion, and Apple Salad

Mango Fool with Chocolate Cookies

DEJEUNER SUR L'HERBE

Chicken Liver-Apple Terrine

Papaya, Red Onion, and Apple Salad

Zucchini Tian with Goat Cheese

Potato Salad with Radicchio

Pears Baked with Cassis

SEASHORE SUPPER

Clams with Pesto

Scallop Terrine with Scallion Sauce

Warm Grilled Vegetables
Maple-Walnut Clafouti with Apples

LABOR DAY LUNCHEON

Walnut-Garlic Dip with Raw Vegetables
Fresh Tomato Tart
Cold Chicken en Gelée
Fresh Ginger Gingerbread

PICNIC ON THE TERRACE

Eggplant with Goat Cheese and Walnuts
Garlic-Basil Shortbreads
Chilled Avocado Soup with Buttermilk
Tomatoes Niçoises
Mushrooms Stuffed with Spinach and Pernod
Upside-down Blueberry Tart

FOURTH OF JULY DINNER

Mushroom-filled Blue Cornmeal Turnovers
*Cream of White Bean Soup with
Roasted Red Pepper Rouille*
Salmon with Soy Sauce and Lime

Scalloped Onions
Tomatoes Baked with Goat Cheese
Poached Meringues in Strawberry Sauce

CINCO DE MAYO SUPPER

Quesadillas with Leeks and Goat Cheese
Black Bean Cakes
Leaf Lettuce with Cayenned Walnuts
Mango Fool

GRADUATION DINNER

Cold Carrot Soup with Guacamole
Lasagne with Chicken and Marsala
Green Bean Salad with Pesto
Upside-down Blueberry Tart

BRIDAL DINNER

Beet Broth with Sour Cream
Fish Mousse with Lobster and Saffron Cream Sauce
Carrot Tart with Spinach "Crust"
Poached Meringues in Strawberry Sauce

SUMMER SUPPER

Eggplant Caviar with Caviar

Chilled Meat Loaf with Chutney

Potato Salad with Radicchio

Papaya, Red Onion, and Apple Salad

Pears Baked with Cassis

WEDDING ANNIVERSARY
DINNER PARTY

Eggplant Caviar with Caviar

Mussels in Saffron Sauce with Zucchini Timbales

Duck with Pears

Turnip Strudel

Fondant of Swiss Chard with Cream

Chocolate Trifle with Raspberries

MAY DAY DINNER

Mâche with Warm Shiitake Mushrooms

Shad Roe with Sorrel Hollandaise

Potatoes with Garlic and Lemon Peel

Walnut Bread Pudding with Apricot Rum Sauce

SUNDAY BRUNCH

Mushrooms Stuffed with Spinach and Pernod
Chicken Liver Soufflé with Fresh Tomato Sauce
Pear Caramel Compote
Fresh Ginger Gingerbread

LENTEN SUPPER

Fish Fillets Broiled with Mustard
Eggplant Baked with Three Cheeses
Potato-Mushroom Gratin
Pear Caramel Compote

EASTER DINNER

Broiled Mushrooms Stuffed with Goat Cheese
Rutabaga-Tomato Soup
Lamb Tarts
Asparagus with Crème Fraîche and Chives
Glazed Onions
Rhubarb Bavarois with Strawberry Sauce

AT-HOME SPA SUPPER

Tomatoes with Balsamic Vinegar and Shallots

Sea Scallops Wrapped in Spinach
Baked Tomatoes Stuffed with Kasha

TWO BUFFET SUPPERS
I.
Turnip Canapés with Chicken and Chutney
Deep-dish Drumstick Pie
Rice with Black-eyed Peas and Sun-dried Tomatoes
Leaf Lettuce with Cayenned Walnuts
Walnut Bread Pudding with Apricot Rum Sauce

II.
Garlic-Basil Shortbreads
Black Bean Chili con Carne
Baked Polenta with Red Peppers
Tomatoes Baked with Goat Cheese
Pears Baked with Cassis

VALENTINE'S DAY DINNER
Cold Beets with Yogurt, Sour Cream, and Dill
Scallop Terrine with Scallion Sauce
Julienned Parsnips and Snow Peas
Cranberry-Apple Streusel

BIRTHDAY DINNER FOR
SOMEONE SPECIAL

Cornmeal Crêpes with Crème Fraîche and Caviar

Carbonnade in Brioches with Tenderloin of Beef

Julienned Parsnips and Snow Peas

Parsley Root Purée

Fresh Orange Cake with Bitter Chocolate Sauce

NEW YEAR'S EVE SUPPER

Cornmeal Crêpes with Crème Fraîche and Caviar

*Duck with Fettuccine, Cracklings, and
Fresh Coriander*

Tomatoes with Balsamic Vinegar and Shallots

Chocolate Trifle with Raspberries

SKI-WEEKEND DINNER

Eggplant-Garlic Soup

*Baked Ziti with Smoked Salmon and
Sun-dried Tomatoes*

Green Bean Salad with Pesto

Pear Caramel Compote

ENGAGEMENT CELEBRATION DINNER

Mushroom-filled Blue Cornmeal Turnovers

Rabbit in White Wine with Fresh Sage

Turnip Strudel

Leaf Lettuce with Cayenned Walnuts

Poached Meringues in Strawberry Sauce

THANKSGIVING DINNER

Corn Chowder with Tarragon

Mâche with Warm Shiitake Mushrooms

Game Hens or Quail with Mole Sauce

Lima Bean Purée with Rosemary and Buttermilk

Carrots with Honey and Fresh Mint

Tomatoes with Balsamic Vinegar and Shallots

Cranberry-Apple Streusel

TWO LOW-FAT DINNERS

I.

Rutabaga-Tomato Soup

Salmon with Soy Sauce and Lime

Julienned Parsnips and Snow Peas

Pears Baked with Cassis

II.

Turnip Canapés with Chicken and Chutney

Fish Fillets with Macadamia Nuts and Guinness

Broccoli with Wasabi

Pear Caramel Compote

COLLEGE REUNION DINNER

Mushroom-filled Blue Cornmeal Turnovers

Arugula Soup

*Curried Shrimp and Chicken with Fresh Mint and
Couscous*

Honey-Quince Tart

CHRISTMAS DINNER

Mushroom Pâté with Black Bean Sauce

Beet Broth with Sour Cream

Duck with Black Pepper and Kumquats

Barley-Leek Gratin

Fondant of Swiss Chard with Cream

Baked Yams with Sour Cream and Chutney

*Cranberry Christmas Pudding with Gingered
Hard Sauce*

SUGGESTED
READING
AND SOURCES

Andoh, Elizabeth. *At Home with Japanese Cooking.* New York: Alfred A. Knopf, 1980.

Beard, James. *American Cookery.* Boston and Toronto: Little Brown & Co., 1972

Brennan, Jennifer. *The Cuisines of Asia.* New York: St. Martin's/ Marek, 1984.

Brennan, Jennifer. *The Original Thai Cookbook.* New York: Richard Marek Publishers, 1981.

Brown, Ellen. *Cooking with the New American Chefs.* New York: Harper & Row, 1985.

Casa, Penelope. *Tapas, the Little Dishes of Spain.* New York: Alfred A. Knopf, 1985.

Chenel, Laura, and Siegfried, Linda. *Chèvre!* Santa Rosa, Calif.: Peaks Pike Publishing Co., 1983.

Clair, Colin. *Kitchen and Table.* New York: Abelard-Schuman Ltd., 1964.

Cronin, Isaac; Harlow, Jay; and Johnson, Paul. *The California Seafood Cook Book.* Berkeley: Aris Books, 1983.

David, Elizabeth. *Classics—Mediterranean Food, French Country Cooking, Summer Cooking.* New York: Alfred A. Knopf, 1980.

FitzGibbon, Theodora. *The Food of the Western World.* New York: Quadrangle/The New York Times Book Co., 1976.

Garmey, Jane. *Great British Cooking—A Well Kept Secret.* New York: Random House, 1981.

Goldberg, Nikki, and Goldberg, David. *The Supermarket Handbook.* New York: Harper & Row, 1971.

Grigson, Jane. *Jane Grigson's Fruit Book.* New York: Atheneum, 1981.

Guerard, Michel. *Michel Guerard's Cuisine Minceur.* New York: William Morrow Inc., 1976.

Hazan, Marcella. *The Classic Italian Cookbook.* New York: Alfred A. Knopf, 1978.

Hazan, Marcella. *More Italian Cooking.* New York: Alfred A. Knopf, 1979.

Heatter, Maida. *Book of Great American Desserts.* New York: Alfred A. Knopf, 1985.

Hillman, Howard. *Great Peasant Dishes of the World.* Boston: Houghton Mifflin Co., 1983.

Jaffrey, Madhur. *An Invitation to Indian Cooking.* New York: Alfred A. Knopf, 1973.

James, Theodore, Jr. *The Gourmet Garden: How to Grow Vegetables, Fruits, and Herbs for Today's Cuisine.* New York: E.P. Dutton, 1983.

Jones, Evan. *American Food.* New York: E.P. Dutton, 1975.

Kennedy, Diana. *The Cuisines of Mexico.* New York: Harper & Row, 1972.

Leung, Mai. *The Chinese People's Cookbook.* New York: Harper & Row, 1979.

Maisner, Heather, ed. *Bon Appétit Country Cooking.* New York: Bonanza Books, 1978.

Mariani, John. *The Dictionary of American Food and Drink.* New York: Ticknor & Fields, 1983.

McPhee, John. *Oranges.* New York: Farrar Straus Giroux, 1967.

Meyers, Perla. *The Peasant Kitchen.* New York: Harper & Row, 1975.

Ngo, Bach. *The Classic Cuisine of Vietnam.* New York: Barron's/Woodbury, 1979.

O'Connor, Hyla. *The Early American Cookbook.* New York: Prentice Hall, 1974.

Penner, Lucille Rect. *The Colonial Cookbook.* New York: Hastings House, 1976.

Prudhomme, Paul. *Chef Paul Prudhomme's Louisiana Kitchen.* New York: William Morrow & Co., 1984.

Rao, Shivaji, and Holkan, Shalini Devi. *Cooking of the Maharajas: The Royal Recipes of India.* New York: The Viking Press, 1975.

Root, Waverly, and Rochmont, Richard. *Eating in America, A History.* Ecco Pr., 1981.

Rosengarten, Frederic, Jr. *The Book of Spices.* Wynnewood, Pa.: Livingston, 1969.

Sokolov, Raymond. *Fading Feast.* New York: Farrar Straus Giroux, 1979.

Tannahill, Reay. *Food in History.* New York: Stein & Day, 1973.

Tarr, Yvonne Young. *The Great East Coast Seafood Book.* New York: Vintage Books/Random House, 1982.

Time-Life Books editors. *The Time-Life American Regional Cookbook.* Boston: Little Brown & Co., 1978.

Trager, James. *Foodbook.* New York: Grossman, 1970.

Trapp, Barbara. *The Modern Art of Chinese Cooking.* New York: William Morrow & Co., 1982.

Tsuji, Shizuo. *Japanese Cooking.* Tokyo, San Francisco, and New York: Kodansha International, 1980.

Volokh, Anne. *The Art of Russian Cuisine.* New York: Macmillan, 1983.

West, Karen. *The Best of Polish Cooking.* New York: Hippocrene Books, 1983.

Wolfert, Paula. *Couscous and Other Good Food from Morocco.* New York: Harper & Row, 1973.

Worthington, Diane Rossen. *The Cuisine of California.* Los Angeles: Jeremy P. Tarcher, 1983.

INDEX